'A book of wise words that will introduce some people to the light, will draw others back to the light, and will itself long shine light in all sorts of unforeseeable and beautiful ways. Every reader can undoubtedly expect to have their own personal epiphany. A brilliant book with an unforgettable message.'

Dr Christine Ranck, co-author of bestselling book
Ignite the Genius Within

'Róisín Fitzpatrick has written a remarkable book that is unique in the annals of near death experiences. Fitzpatrick describes her own harrowing brush with death and transcendent near death experience, and guides us through her discovery of the forerunners of NDEs in the ancient roots of pre-Celtic culture. Experiences like Róisín's have now been validated by hundreds of scientific studies around the world, and provide evidence that consciousness is more than the brain and indeed that we are more than our bodies. As a guide to enhancing your own spirituality, *Taking Heaven Lightly* is a love story in the most sublime sense.'

Dr Bruce Greyson, co-editor of *The Handbook of Near Death Experiences: Thirty Years of Investigation*

'A very important and poignant personal account of her near death experience, exploring among other things ancient Irish mythology and megalithic monuments. Róisín Fitzpatrick presents fascinating insights into Newgrange and its associated mythology, suggesting access to a heavenly realm, and brings a real relevance from this ancient culture for modern times.'

Anthony Murphy, author of
Newgrange: Monument to Immortality

Róisín Fitzpatrick is a graduate of Trinity College Dublin and the University of Geneva where she specialised in Business and International Relations. Speaking both French and Italian, she worked for a short time at the European Commission and United Nations before receiving a tenured position at the European Bank for Reconstruction and Development. Later in her life, after overcoming a debilitating illness, brain haemorrhage and near death experience, Róisín turned these adversities into a positive life change.

Passionate about sharing the beauty of the light from her near death experience, in a way that people can connect with their own inner light, she was inspired to create a series of contemporary artworks – the Artist of the Light collection. Róisín's primary intention through this art is to enhance well-being in both residential and corporate environments. Róisín exhibits regularly on both sides of the Atlantic, with over ten exhibitions in the US over the past few years in Manhattan, Washington D.C. and the greater Boston area. Her work is on permanent display at The Irish American Heritage Museum in upstate New York, Glucksman Ireland House in Manhattan, Anam Cara Gallery in Connecticut and the National Concert Hall in Dublin.

Roisin's art has been endorsed by Deepak Chopra, Marianne Williamson, Roma Downey, Mark Burnett, and critically acclaimed by *Forbes*, *The Wall Street Journal*, *The Washington Post*, *Boston Globe*, *Artnews*, *IN New York*, *WHERE New York*, *Irish Arts Review*, *The Irish Times*, *Irish Independent*, *Irish America Magazine*, *Irish Examiner USA* and *The Irish Voice*. *Taking Heaven Lightly* is her first book.

Taking Heaven Lightly

RÓISÍN FITZPATRICK

HACHETTE
BOOKS
IRELAND

First published in 2015 by Hachette Books Ireland
First published in paperback in 2016

A CIP catalogue record for this title is available from the British Library

ISBN 9781473614161

Printed and bound by Clays Ltd, St Ives plc

Hachette Books Ireland policy is to use papers that are natural, renewable
and recyclable products and made from wood grown in sustainable forests.
The logging and manufacturing processes are expected to conform to the
environmental regulations of the country of origin.

Hachette Books Ireland
8 Castlecourt Centre
Castleknock
Dublin 15, Ireland

A division of Hachette UK Ltd.
Carmelite House
50 Victoria Embankment
London EC47 0DZ

www.hachette.ie

I dedicate this book to you. I share my story so that you may tap into your infinite potential and become the person you were born to be. It is not necessary to have a life-threatening near death experience to feel this love in your life. All that is required is a willingness to be open to the possibility of a greater existence beyond this physical realm, and then to be guided on your own unique soul's journey. My wish for you is to experience inner peace, love and joy in your life. This is the essential truth of who you are. This is available to you right here, right now, if you make the choice to take your first step towards the light ...

A human being is part of a whole, called by us the Universe – a part limited in time and space. He experiences himself, his thoughts, and feelings, as something separated from the rest – a kind of optical delusion of his consciousness. This delusion is a kind of prison for us, restricting us to our personal desires and to affection for a few persons nearest us. Our task must be to free ourselves from this prison by widening our circles of compassion to embrace all living creatures and the whole of nature in its beauty.

Albert Einstein

CONTENTS

PROLOGUE

NEAR DEATH EXPERIENCE AND CONFIRMATION BY A MEDICAL EXPERT

In one instant, on 22 March 2004, my world was changed forever. Without any warning, I suddenly found myself in a situation where my life was in danger when I suffered a subarachnoid brain haemorrhage.

Later, as I lay in the ICU, fully aware of the potential risks, I embarked on the most remarkable journey of my life – a near death experience (NDE). During this life-transforming journey beyond the physical realm, I experienced a sense of blissful unity with the universe, and glimpsed the beauty of the afterlife. Ironically, the thing that brought me closest to death became the conduit for the most powerful source of my healing: connecting to an eternal light which, I came to understand, is available to us all, should we choose it.

Exactly nine years to the day after my brain haemorrhage, I met with Dr Bruce Greyson, one of the pioneers and medical experts in near death experience (NDE) research in the United States.[1] Dr Greyson had approached me a couple of years earlier after he heard about my work as Artist of the Light, from a mutual acquaintance. He had asked me to become a participant in his studies because he was interested to learn more about my NDE. Through this research process, I had completed numerous forms and questionnaires as he had analysed my NDE from every angle. When I travelled to see him in person that day at the University of Virginia in Charlottesville, I went in search of the answer to one question: did I have a near death experience during my brain haemorrhage?

I sought an objective opinion from this internationally recognised expert because I wanted to know if the extraordinary event which had such a profound impact on my life, and my whole new way of being, was indeed a near death experience.

I remember sitting in his office on a bright morning in March as the early sunlight streamed through the windows. The walls of his office were surrounded by rows of beige filing cabinets all stacked tightly together and filled to the brim with research he had compiled over 40 years. I sat comfortably in a cushioned seat, feeling a combination of eager anticipation for our pending conversation and gratitude for his generosity in spending this time with me.

Although we had corresponded through email and

letters, this was our first meeting in person. As soon as I met Dr Greyson, I immediately felt at ease in his presence. My first impression was of a man who looks much younger than his years, as he radiated a warm smile. When we spoke to each other I realised that he has a special way of understanding people, with genuine compassion and empathy.

While sitting in Dr Greyson's office, he answered my queries about various aspects of NDEs in general and then listened attentively when I described the details of my own personal experience. I struggled to find the exact words to describe the beauty of my experience because we simply don't have the language for euphoric love, brilliance of light and all-encompassing serenity. Nonetheless, I brought him through every detail of my experience. I related how, during my brain haemorrhage, I had embarked on the greatest journey of my life, which radically shifted my whole perception of life and death.

I continued to explain that, after that day, my whole life was turned upside down, or to be more accurate, right side up. Everything that I thought was real before paled into insignificance, as an entirely new perception of life appeared before me. I shared how my NDE shook the very foundations of my existence, altering my view of myself and of this world. In a very real sense, after my near death experience, I gained a new appreciation for life.

After speaking together for a long while, he smiled at me as he paused for a moment, then he leaned forward and said, 'It always amazes me how so many years after the NDE, experiencers can relate every single detail of the experience, as if it has just occurred. I can confirm that you had an NDE when your life was in danger. I know this because in addition to your high score on the NDE scale in my research, your whole persona, how you live in this world, your attitudes, beliefs and values are all fully consistent with a person who has undergone this traumatic change in life. Your life's journey over the past nine years reflects this transformation.'

Looking directly at me, Dr Greyson continued, 'From your experience you have something valuable to share with people who are searching to find a meaning in life and a purpose for our existence. Many are looking for something deeper, wishing to find more joy and inner peace. Some may even yearn for a Divine loving connection, which at some level we know exists but at times seems to be elusive and beyond our grasp. You can encourage people to access this love and fully embrace life.'

'You also have something quite unique to share. We have a tendency to look to the older Eastern cultures for an explanation and understanding of death with books such as the *Tibetan Book of the Dead*. With your Irish heritage, you can ground your experience in the timeless wisdom of an ancient Western culture in a way that is relevant to our modern lives.

Through changing our perception of death, we can shed many of our fears and become free to live life from love instead of fear. This is how you can contribute, Róisín. Write this book.'

My sincerest thanks to Dr Greyson for playing a pivotal role in encouraging me to take a conceptual dream and turn it into this book. In the following pages, I recount the story of my own life leading up to my NDE, through the experience and to the present. I share the tremendous impact that the NDE has had on my view of this world, since I had the chance to glimpse what lies beyond in the 'next' realm.

During my NDE I discovered that 'Heaven' is an exquisite state of pure love that lies at the very core of our beings, while simultaneously existing beyond any boundaries of time and space. I understand it may sound naive, or even ludicrous, to write of such love when we are surrounded by so much destructive chaos and violence in this world. Yet I also know, in my soul, that this love is accessible. *You do not need to have an NDE to feel this in your own life. I invite you to open up to the possibility of the existence of this love and you may just find that you can not only feel this love but actually integrate it into your daily life.*

Many people, perhaps even you, have encountered a myriad of difficult challenges and hardships along the path of life, maybe in early childhood, teenage years or later on. As a result, maybe you are still searching to find happiness, a sense of purpose and love, to create a better future than past. This might even be the reason why this book is in your hands right now.

I invite you to join me on the soul's journey to reconnect with our deepest truth: *we are pure love and eternal light.*

This Divine Light lies within each and every one of us. We have simply forgotten how empowered we truly are.[2]

If you wish to explore this further, parts 2 and 3 of the book provide techniques for strengthening your connection with the Divine Light in your own life. Irrespective of the challenging trials and tribulations you encounter on life's journey, you can always make the choice to experience greater joy and love in your life now.

> *Life is no 'brief candle' to me.*
> *It is a sort of splendid torch*
> *Which I have got hold of for a*
> *Moment, and I want to make*
> *It burn as brightly as possible*
> *Before handing it on*
> *To future generations.*
>   George Bernard Shaw

PART 1:

SEARCHING FOR AND FINDING LOVE WITHIN: LIFE BEFORE AND AFTER MY NEAR DEATH EXPERIENCE

CHAPTER I

GIFT OF LIFE: HAPPY CHILDHOOD ... AND A BIG QUESTION

My mother often joked that if she had stayed in the west of Ireland, where she was reared, she would have turned to rust with all the rain. Radiating life through her clear blue eyes, soft blonde curls and gentle smile, her beauty along with her effervescent personality were a winning combination, and my father simply adored her.

Dad grew up across the country from my mother's birthplace, on the east coast of Ireland, in County Dublin. He was one in a million: a kind-spirited person with a mischievous, hilarious sense of humour. Although he was a gifted athlete at golf, tennis and rugby, standing almost six feet tall, with thick, wavy, jet-black hair, his greatest achievement of all was being a devoted husband to my mother and loving father of our family.

My parents were introduced by a mutual friend while on vacation at the coastal resort of Kilkee in County Clare. After spending just a few days together, they fell in love and became engaged. Five months later, their wedding took place on 8 January 1958. This was the beginning of a happy married life that lasted nearly 53 years.

My parents had four daughters. I am the youngest. My sisters were all born two years apart; then I unexpectedly came along five years later. Being born a son would have been a redeeming feature, so much so that for months my sisters were told they were going to have a baby brother. The day of my birth, one of my sisters proudly announced to her school teacher and the whole class that her baby brother, Brian, was going to be born that day. She still jokes with me of her embarrassment at having to go back to school the following day to say, 'It's a girl.' They named me Róisín (pronounced *Ro-sheen*), which means 'Little Rose' in Irish.

Our home was a happy home, with a constant flow of friends and family passing through for chats over cups of tea, and to enjoy Mum's baking. The aroma of freshly baked brown bread and crispy apple tarts wafted through the kitchen on a daily basis. During the late summer months, the countertops were packed with a colourful array of jars filled to the brim with homemade fruit jams in preparation for the long winter months. Mum was a Home Economics teacher and we were her most willing students – and expert tasters!

My paternal grandfather established a retail shoe company in Dublin in 1926. Of his seven children, his three sons continued to grow the business. Dad was a company director and buyer. He was often referred to as 'the gentleman of the shoe business' in Ireland by his colleagues in the trade, and he truly was. In 1978, the family business was divided among the brothers. Though Dad was of an age when many people consider retiring, instead he set up his own retail shoe company. Mum was a tremendous support to him. They dedicated themselves to establishing their own shoe shop, on Grafton Street, the main retail street in Dublin.

From the age of nine, I often visited the shop with Mum and was delighted when given some simple tasks to do. I was like a kid in a sweetshop wide-eyed with glee, while surrounded by a vast array of beautiful shoes all day. I loved searching for the smallest sizes I could find and trying them on in all the various styles and colours. With a couple of inches to spare, my small feet barely kept the shoes on, as I flip-flopped around on the tan-coloured linoleum of the stock-room floor.

When I was a little girl, I used to sit on the sheepskin rug which lay on the floor in our family's sitting room, next to the corner of Dad's armchair. I remember one day we were watching a show called *Come Dancing*, a forerunner to the celebrity dance shows on television now. I asked Dad if he could dance as well as the performers on the show. He told me, 'No, Róisín, I have two left feet.' I looked up at him, looked down at his feet and looked up at him again and said earnestly, 'I see why you are in the shoe business, Dad, but I will keep your secret.' For years, I genuinely thought that my dearest Dad had two left feet!

As I grew older, I enjoyed working in the shop and was often there on Saturdays and during the summer and Christmas sales. There was a great atmosphere and sense of fun among staff, who loved nothing more than playing practical jokes on the new junior members. Invariably, they would end up in Dad's office, searching for the tin of 'elbow grease', or sent into Bewley's bakery next door looking for the 'pregnant tart'. I had heard of these tricks, so I was lucky to escape the embarrassment.

I had a happy childhood, attending the local school from the age of four to seventeen, where I was educated by some wonderful teachers. But the greatest education of all was out in nature and most especially on the grounds of Howth Castle, located just a stone's throw from my home. After school during the autumn months, my best friend Michele and I often picked blackberries near the forest around the castle. In the winter, if we were lucky enough to have days off school due to heavy snowfalls, we headed to the castle grounds with our old turf bags slung over our shoulders. Previously used for carrying turf that we burned at home, the bags now served their real purpose, as sturdy sledges for sliding down the snow-covered hills on, again and again and again, until dusk descended. With ice frozen in the creases of our corduroy trousers, red raw hands and ruddy smiling faces, we headed home, praying for the white flurries to swirl and fall throughout the night so we could continue our escapades the following day on a fresh blanket of snow.

We also loved exploring the mysteries of another world

in the forest on the grounds of Howth Castle. The beech and sycamore trees, regal in stature with a strong presence yet gentle nature, welcomed us with smiling faces embedded in the crevices and cracks of the warm bark.

As the sunlight filtered through a canopy of leaves, the beams of light revealed a concealed Neolithic (New Stone Age) dolmen: surrounded by soft ferns and long grass, this stone structure, which is over 5,500 years old, consists of numerous vertical slab stones with an enormous horizontal rock placed on top. Even though the overall structure has collapsed, possibly due to the pressure and weight of the capstone, this old ruin has managed to maintain its majestic glory. It still looks like a stone table built for giants, albeit a lopsided one![3]

We clambered all over, in and around these huge stones, with our blue-and-white check gingham skirts peeping in and out of visibility. The warm outer stones of this dolmen embraced us, inviting us to enter into the cooler inner sanctuary. With a musty scent in the air, the moist moss and lichen-covered rocks hummed with a faint whisper. A barely audible, rhythmic vibration pulsated throughout the site, as if Mother Nature were breathing life into this sacred womb.

As a child, my senses were instinctively attuned to the high-level vibrations that exist in this ancient place. That was before I grew up and became a so-called 'sensible' adult, where reason and logic overruled my intuition. It was only many years later, after numerous life experiences, most especially a powerful, life-changing near death experience NDE, that I learned to fully

appreciate the wisdom of this magical place. I finally
heard and felt the true power of that sacred message.

After my near death experience (NDE), I took the time to
look at all aspects of my life and what was really important.
I felt such a huge sense of gratitude for being alive, and I
wished to thank the people who had shown me kindness.
I contacted my favourite primary school teacher who had
taught me when I was seven or eight years old. When I
took her out for lunch I realised in seeing her again just
what an important inspiration she had always been to me.
Yes, she taught me maths, spelling and drawing, but more
importantly, her essence was of pure love. She saw the best
in each child and brought it to the surface. This reunion
was a lovely opportunity to thank her in person.

My Granny Fitzpatrick was also hugely influential in
my childhood. Luckily, she lived close to our home so we
were able to visit her regularly. I remember scampering
up the stairs in my enthusiasm to see her. However, I was
always stopped in my tracks on the landing half way up
the stairs by a plethora of stunning shades of light which
poured through an enormous stained glass window.

As the light shone through the glass it created a
magical array of cobalt blue, crimson red and golden
yellow which reflected off the walls and carpet, covering
my body. I used to stand there transfixed in awe, staring
at this beautiful light, and when I moved, the colours
flowed and swayed with me as part of a mystical dance
with light. 'Róisín, Granny's waiting for you,' Dad
would call in his gentle voice. As I continued bounding
up the stairs to reach Granny's bedroom, I knew that

my ethereal dance was only paused for a while, to recommence on my next visit. Little did I know at the time that this early childhood experience would be a catalyst for working with glass and light later in my life.

With the amber coals radiating warmth from the open fire, Granny would sit with her two little black and brown dachshunds at her feet. I would scramble onto the soft woollen rug on her lap as she swayed back and forth in her rocking chair. When she enjoyed herself, her giggly laugh became contagious, as Dad and I would also invariably end up laughing uncontrollably. She had a special 'energy' that I was not able to articulate in words. All I knew was that it was a great joy to be with her; I simply loved being around her.

Then one day when I was seven years of age, Mum collected us from school and told us that Granny had gone to Heaven. Although I cried when I heard that she was gone, I felt inexplicably calm because I could sense a warm presence enveloping me. Even though I could not understand it, I was still able to somehow feel Granny's love and connect with her.

Throughout my childhood, I received a tremendous amount of love from my parents and sisters. Fortunate to grow up in a happy and stable home, I was blessed in that I never wanted for anything, and was provided with every opportunity in life. Although I received all of this unconditionally, at a deeper level, being the youngest child by five years in an Irish Catholic family, I always felt that I should never have been born.

Of course, I am just one of many 'surprises' born onto this planet. I have heard of other people also experiencing a deep feeling that they should not be here. Some people who feel out of place on this earth question their very existence. Others search endlessly, trying to make sense of life.

I experienced this sense of not belonging as a lack, so I compensated by trying to excel in my studies and proving my independence. I searched from the outside for the sense of self-worth that could only ever come from within. In the process of seeking externally, I gradually lost the connection with my inner self. Thus as I grew older, I grew the *very opposite* of wiser!

Over the years, I distanced myself further and further from my soul by allowing objective reasoning to overshadow my inner knowing or intuition. For example, due to the suffering portrayed in the media from the conflict in Northern Ireland I developed a confused view of religion because, in my mind, this seemed to be the reason why they were always at war. This violence, which was ostensibly in the name of religion, made no sense to me. How could they murder each other when both sides claimed to be 'Christian', with a belief in the Commandment, 'Thou shalt not kill'? As a consequence, I lost all my faith in God. Similarly, I rejected the mysticism of Celtic lore, which I had become familiar with in my youth – to my reason-focused brain, the possibility of life beyond the material world appeared too unrealistic to comprehend. It took many years and life experiences before I learned to fully appreciate the true meaning.

I have since come to learn, especially when I experienced a life-altering NDE, that at a deeper soul level each one of us is born for a reason. Everyone's life has meaning and value. Each person has a purpose, even if at times we may question why we are here. As we journey on life's path, we are given innumerable opportunities to connect with our souls' deepest truths to become the people we were born to be.

When I was in secondary school, I enjoyed learning but I could not wait to leave and get out into the world. I was delighted when I was accepted into Trinity College Dublin. Trinity is a special place to study, situated right in the heart of Dublin city. Once you walk through the entrance at Front Arch, all the hustle and bustle of the city centre is left behind, as you enter another world – a scholarly sanctuary. The university is steeped in history, being over 400 years old, with a long and rich history of traditions and beautiful architecture.

The university is famous as the home for the *Book of Kells*, the illuminated manuscript of the Gospels, transcribed by the monks in the seventh century. During my four years studying at Trinity, I was asked on numerous occasions for directions by tourists searching for 'Kelly's novel'. Somehow I don't think the medieval monks would have appreciated this modern moniker for their sacred script!

I remember standing in the hallway of my parents' home at the end of my first year at Trinity. Suitcase in hand, I was about to head off for the summer, having received a scholarship to study Italian at the University of Siena. Of course I was scared, but I took a deep breath and decided to jump at the opportunity. I felt just the same sense of nervous excitement the next summer before I left to work in the United States. It was a similar feeling in the summer of third year, when I went abroad once more, this time to work in Canada.

In all of these life-changing experiences, though each could feel nerve-racking at the time because I hardly knew anyone or anything about the places I was going to, looking back I invariably met wonderful people while travelling in different countries. These experiences would help me in later years when I needed to take other leaps of faith.

In my third year at Trinity, I was given the opportunity to study for six months at the university of Louvain-la-Neuve in Belgium. While studying there I lived in a mixed-gender students' residence where everyone got on like a house on fire. I learned that total immersion really is the best way to learn a language. By the end of the six months, I was not only speaking and writing in French, I was even dreaming in French. However, the learning process was not without its faux pas. I remember saying to everyone at dinner one evening that Irish food was different to Belgian, as we have '*pas de préservatif*', thinking I was saying there were no preservatives in Irish food. Little did I know, until they all fell around laughing, that I had just told them there were no condoms in Irish food! Another time, I announced to everyone that I was off to the chemist to get some batteries, or so I thought. Alas, no, I had just told them that I was off to the chemist to buy *pilule*, which is French for the contraceptive pill. All the guys were grinning from ear to ear. As a naive young Irish girl, I was simply mortified.

After graduating from Trinity in 1990, I was among the lucky graduates chosen for a six-month work programme at the European Commission in Brussels. During this period, I travelled to many of the countries which had recently regained their freedom after years of oppression behind the Iron Curtain. I was thankful for the opportunity to expand my vision and learn so much about the different European countries.

In addition to travelling around Europe, I visited Japan for three weeks as part of a programme sponsored by the Japanese government in conjunction with the European Commission. We travelled to Mount Fuji and wrote our requests at the Buddhist temples. In Kyoto, we saw the spectacular Golden Temple and Japanese Zen Gardens. I distinctly remember experiencing a sense of calm in these places. Although at this point in my life I did not believe in God, nor in the possibility of a spiritual force guiding the universe, nonetheless, I was still intrigued by the Shinto faith. I was fascinated to learn about the similarity between this religious system and many of the old Irish beliefs in terms of the reverence for nature. A few days later on the same trip I watched a kodo drumming performance. This primal art form resonated with me as it reminded me of some Celtic spiritual traditions. Unconsciously, something began to stir within me, suggesting that there might be more to life than is visible to the eye.

However, this light was quickly extinguished when I had a hauntingly powerful experience while standing at the peace memorial in downtown Hiroshima. A spindly steel skeleton of a structure is all that remains of the Dome – it was all but destroyed, along with most of the city and its inhabitants, by the nuclear bomb in August 1945. The shell of this edifice stands isolated, surrounded by an eerie silence. After learning of the devastating effect of the Second World War on so many different populations around the world, and seeing the photographs and papers in Hiroshima Museum, I remember thinking: how can the human race intentionally destroy itself? How could there be a loving God, with all this devastation and destruction?

On my return from Japan, my work at the European Commission came to an end. At this point, I was fortunate to receive a scholarship from the Swiss government to study at the University of Geneva's graduate programme of International Relations – *Hautes Études Internationales*. I was delighted to have the opportunity to learn more about world politics and economics, as I tried to make some rational sense of this world in which we all live.

When I had completed my studies and was about to graduate at the end of the academic year, one of my professors invited me to work for his department at the United Nations (UN) in Geneva for the summer.

In the midst of this broadening experience, one of my other professors called me into her office and explained that she had just received a request from the newly established European Bank for Reconstruction and Development in London. This bank was created to assist the former communist countries of Eastern Europe with their economic integration into the rest of Europe. They had contacted her in their search for a Business and Economics graduate, fluent in French and English, to liaise with the European Commission. Smiling, she said, 'The job description is identical to your resumé, Róisín, the only detail missing is your name!'

After applying for the position, I was called for interviews in London. I remember that, on the day prior to the interviews, I had my hair tied up in a twisted, sophisticated style, in an attempt to look older than my years, because I was only 23 at the time. In the hair salon they must have used an entire can of hairspray, as my abiding memory of the series of interviews was of being in a tiny room and thinking that I must be 'gassing' them with the hair spray. The fumes must have worked however, because they offered me the job!

Within a week, I received the formal contract in the mail. On the crisp white headed paper with the European Bank's royal blue logo, the detailed terms of my tenured position were clearly typed in black ink. I had been offered a full-time, life-long contract, with all the financial perks of expatriate status, to work for one of the most prestigious international institutions. This was an incredible opportunity for somebody so young.

These contracts were like gold dust. So why did I feel sick to my core? Why did I have an awful sinking feeling in the pit of my stomach? Why was I postponing signing the contract that I should have been jumping for joy at receiving? In retrospect I can see that my inner voice, instinct, soul or whatever you might wish to call it – that part of us that is always connected with our highest truth – was whispering to me, 'This *is* a great job, Róisín, *but it is not right for you.*' Rationally, it made sense to take this job because on paper it seemed perfect. Choosing reason over intuition, I ignored my inner knowing. After signing the contract, I packed my few boxes and headed off to London at the end of the summer. This also meant splitting up with a wonderful Swedish student whom I had been dating at the time. He was so supportive and encouraged me to take the job because he knew that this was a great opportunity.

At one level, I was extremely grateful for this job because Ireland was in a dire economic situation in the early 1990s and many of my classmates from university were unable to find work. I also felt that it was a great privilege to work using my skills in an international context and hoped to make some positive, even if minor, difference to the quality of people's lives in Eastern Europe. I recall laughing with Mum on the phone, relaying to her the health insurance component of my contract. 'Goodness, Mum, as if I would ever need that!' I had always enjoyed great health. However, little did I know what the future held in store for me.

❂ ❂ ❂

For the first few weeks in Britain, I stayed at a friend's apartment in south London. Once I knew my way around the city, I rented an apartment on the first floor of an old period building which was nestled on Meard Street, a little cobblestoned lane in the heart of London's West End. It was an atmospheric place with lots of people bustling around the theatre district at night. There was, however, one disadvantage to living in this apartment.

Within a couple of weeks of moving in, some rather dubious characters began to ring my buzzer late at night. Although initially perplexed by these intrusions, I soon realised while perusing a guide book of this area of central London that the first-floor apartments on my street were rented by the more expensive 'ladies of the night'! I immediately ran down the flight of stairs, tore away the label with my name on the bell and replaced it with a 'Don't even think about ringing this bell' note, which thankfully worked – most of the time.

It was fantastic to be located in such a central location. I was able to take the iconic red double-decker London bus to work and be there in about ten minutes. Every morning I watched the number eight red bus trundle down Oxford Street, slow down and eventually grind to a halt at the bus stop. I grabbed onto the metal pole and stepped aboard through the open doorway located at the rear of the bus.

'Where ye off t', luv?' the conductor always asked in his distinctive Cockney accent. 'Bishopsgate,' I'd reply, all the while smiling at the conductor and maintaining eye contact to ensure that I was polite. By saying as little as possible, I could be taken for British, American or from mainland Europe, but as soon as I spoke, my accent could reveal my origins. Every morning was the same, as I gave a monosyllabic answer in a hushed tone.

I was very much aware of my Irish accent. It was a challenging time to be Irish in London, as the Irish Republican Army (IRA) was at the height of conducting its bombing campaign in the City of London's financial district. It had only been a few months before I arrived in London that, in April 1992, a massive one-ton bomb detonated by the IRA at the Baltic Exchange struck a costly blow to the heart of the United Kingdom's financial district.

The worst losses were the three fatalities and 91 injuries,[4] but the bomb also caused £800 million worth of damage, significantly more than the total damage caused by the 10,000 explosions that had occurred in Northern Ireland since the beginning of 'the Troubles' in 1969.[5]

One year later, on Saturday, 24 April 1993, at 10.27 a.m., without any warning, there was a loud blast in the City of London. At that moment, I was in the centre of the financial district, attending the European Bank's annual general meeting. The conference room was packed with delegates from the bank and representatives from all the countries of Eastern Europe. The violent intensity of the explosion caused all of the glass windows to shudder in their frames, rattling in unison. This was quickly followed by a huge rush of air which swept through the room, engulfing the entire space. We all gasped, as we sat motionless holding our breaths, not knowing what would happen next.

Staring at each other with disbelief, we quickly realised that a bomb had just been detonated nearby.

The one-ton bomb had exploded in the major Bishopsgate thoroughfare of the financial district. This massive bomb caused extensive damage to multiple buildings up to a third of a mile away from the centre of the blast, including London's tallest building at that time, the NatWest Tower.

Shaken by the incident, I decided to head straight home rather than returning to my office. Without speaking a word to anyone en route, I walked the few miles back to my apartment. Making my way past the cordoned-off areas, where the air was heavy with clouds of dingy, dark fragments of dust, I carefully selected my steps to avoid the pointed shards of glass and jagged slabs of concrete. Littered among the debris were papers and documents strewn in every direction, expulsed from the gaping voids that only hours earlier were securely sealed office windows.

When I eventually arrived at my apartment, there were a number of frantic messages on my answering machine from my Irish friend Séamus, who also lived in London. He knew that I was working that day in the financial district. Frightened that I might have been injured by the blast, as soon as I replayed the messages I heard, 'Róisín, are you OK? Call me as soon as you get this message. I have been trying to get hold of you at your office, but they do not know where you are. Call me.'

I phoned him immediately. 'Thanks a million, Séamus, I'm fine. Thank goodness it was a Saturday, and most of the offices were empty, otherwise it would have been a massacre.'[6]

After these bomb attacks, the British government tightened security, creating a 'ring of steel' around London's financial district, whereby access routes to the financial hub were either closed off or secured by checkpoints with armed policemen. The IRA maintained the atmosphere of fear by issuing a statement: 'No one should be misled into underestimating the IRA's intention to mount future planned attacks into the political and financial heart of the British state ... In the context of present political realities, further attacks on the City of London and elsewhere are inevitable.'[7]

The pressures of being Irish while living in London were not my only challenges during this period. At the time when I was working at the European Bank, I was at least ten years younger than my peers and felt totally out of my depth. However, by focusing on the positives, I tried to make the best of my new job. I would often work late into the night, as there was so much to complete. One of my colleagues joked that I should have had a sleeping bag rolled up under my desk, so I could just keep going from one day into the next. Nobody forced me to work that hard; it was my own choice. Looking back at that time of my life, through a combination of perfectionism and over-working, I masked my real feelings and ignored my soul's truth.

A friend of mine once said that working in a job that is well paid, but in an environment that is not true to your soul, is like being a bird trapped in a golden cage. While the surroundings and the exterior may look great and while materially such a position may fulfil all the requirements that society associates with success, nonetheless, if it is not *your truth*, it does not matter if it is a golden one: a cage is still a cage. In the hidden recesses of my heart, I knew that working at the European Bank was not my truth. I felt like the trapped bird. I was imprisoned in the golden cage. I continued on persisting with sheer mental determination, trying to make it work against my inner guidance and the wisdom of my soul.

One way of trying to relieve some of the stress and tension from over-working was to spend time with my friends. As part of my role at the European Bank, I travelled regularly to Brussels. When it was possible, I planned the meetings for either early or late in the week, so that I could catch up with my pals over the weekends. I was grateful to my friend Eric for his warm welcome to his home. He helped me through this difficult time in my life by always encouraging me to stay positive, even when I was struggling.

Rather than staying in an impersonal hotel, I preferred to sleep on the floor in Eric's apartment. One evening, after enjoying the company of some friends, I returned to Eric's apartment in the wee hours of the morning. Tip-toeing around so as not to disturb him from his sleep, I fumbled around in the dark as I did not wish to turn the light on and accidentally wake him. Eric's apartment was tiny, consisting of one room with a sink for a kitchen, and the bathroom was barely a corner of the room, with a curtain for a door. So, in the faint, hazy glow of the streetlights, I grabbed what I thought was toothpaste and began brushing my teeth. Instantly, I realised that it was an ointment used for relieving muscle spasms through the generation of heat. Within seconds I transformed into a fire-breathing dragon, screaming at the top of my lungs. Eric woke up and switched on the light. I whipped the curtain back and stared at him, foaming at the mouth, toothbrush in one hand and tube of muscle relaxant in the other. I can still see the look on his face as he rolled around laughing. One thing was for sure: if nothing else, it certainly took my mind off work.

In addition to representing the European Bank at conferences throughout Europe and liaising with the European Commission, I was one of the main organisers for a conference in Mexico. The convention was hosted by the President of Mexico, with the objective of assisting government officials of Eastern Europe with their economic transition. There was a huge amount of work involved to ensure that everything flowed smoothly.

After returning from the conference, my time at the European Bank became increasingly stressful. Working around the clock began to take its toll. I became weaker and it took more and more caffeine to keep me going. Even though I had been careful with the food I ate when I was in Mexico, I still became ill with food poisoning. I had picked up a parasitic infection called giardiasis, but I was unaware of this at the time. Having never been seriously ill before, I had always taken my good health for granted. As a consequence, I just kept working as hard as ever, not giving my body a chance to recover. This marked the start of my health problems.

When I was working at the European Bank, one of my colleagues was a wonderful British woman, Heather Altland de Diaz. Heather is a force of nature. With all the character of her father, a Royal Navy commander, and her stalwart mother, she has a charismatic presence. One Friday evening as we were leaving work together, I told her that I was going home to Ireland for the weekend. We chatted as we took the short stroll together to Liverpool Street train station. I was seriously ill by this time but still in denial and battling on.

As I boarded the train, she called out in full voice, in her beautifully enunciated English, 'Róisín, be sure to sit near that good-looking chap, won't you now, daaahling?' Mortified, I sat down on the only seat available in the carriage, directly opposite this handsome young man who was staring straight at me. Yes, Heather was right, he was easy on the eye, but I wanted the ground to open up and swallow me. To avoid any conversation, I diverted my gaze to watch Heather smiling and waving as the train pulled out of the station. I knew she could see that I was finding everything extremely challenging at work and she was trying to lift my spirits.

Around this time, I remember a friend of mine commented that I looked very pale and recommended that I be tested for mononucleosis. When the result came back negative, I felt obliged to continue working, as the doctors could not identify any specific illness. What I did not realise was that the mononucleosis test is notorious for returning a false negative when the disease is early in its course. I continued working, getting weaker and weaker every day, for another six months.

I also developed a piercing pain inside my right ear, as if a surgeon's scalpel were constantly scraping, scouring and scratching. I seemed to have a permanent infection, even after several courses of antibiotics. No matter what medication I took, the abrasive pain grated on every nerve, making it almost impossible to sleep.

I travelled home quite regularly, at least once a month. Mum and Dad could see me getting weaker with each visit. Dad told me later that he truly regretted not intervening: he wanted me to just stop everything. Even if he had tried, I am sure that I would not have heard him. Whatever I felt about the deafening pain in my ear, I have also inherited a combination of my mother's west of Ireland indomitable spirit and my father's stubborn Fitzpatrick streak – which of course he absolutely insisted that he never had – so there was not a hope that I would have listened!

As my condition worsened, I went out for dinner one weekend with my friend Séamus. Huddled together at a corner table of the restaurant, I cried my eyes out for the entire meal. Poor Séamus withstood all the glares from people around us who assumed that we were in a relationship and he was somehow being horrible to me. This could not have been further from the truth. He was incredibly supportive and kind.

By December 1993, I had been ill for over a year. Late one night, as I walked home from work through the dimly lit London streets, I gradually lost all power in my limbs and eventually collapsed outside a corner shop a few streets away from my home. I lay motionless in a crumpled heap on the pavement, my black coat crushed against the damp concrete and my leather briefcase strewn before me. I was so weak that I could not lift myself up. Every time I tried to stir, the movements were futile, as I repeatedly crashed to the ground again and again.

Then a complete stranger appeared from nowhere, offering to bring me to wherever I needed to go. Initially, I declined this man's kind offer of assistance until it quickly dawned on me that I desperately needed his help. As he pulled me up I was unable to stand, let alone walk, so he picked me up and carried me in his arms. Hurried passers-by brushed against us, noisily shouting at each other, revelling in their night out in the West End, but I barely spoke a word other than to give directions. When we arrived at the main entrance of my building, he offered to carry me up the one flight of stairs to my apartment, but I insisted that I was fine.

'Thank you, thank you, thank you,' I sighed, relieved to have made it home.

As I reached out to close the front door behind me, I glanced down the street and realised that just as suddenly as he had appeared, he disappeared down the winding cobbled pathway of Meard Street. Even though at that time I had no belief whatsoever in anything beyond the material realm, looking back, I can see that this man who had appeared for me was a living angel. Whether real or ethereal, I am not sure how I would have managed without his assistance that night.

It must have taken me half an hour on my hands and knees as I hauled my body, one step at a time, up the single flight of stairs, my face rubbing off the harsh grey carpet with my briefcase trailing behind me. I eventually arrived at my front door and admitted defeat. The battle was over. I could continue no longer.

That night after I dozed off to sleep, without warning, I abruptly found myself out of my body and floating near the ceiling above the foot of my bed. From that vantage point, I scanned the bedroom, looking at the pinewood panelling on the walls and worn beige carpet on the floor. As I hovered freely, I was surprised to see my body below me on the mattress, lying limp and lifeless. I distinctly remember that my ashen face was gaunt and pale, as it protruded from under the creased midnight-blue duvet cover. I felt calm as I surveyed the whole scene. There was a quiet silence. I had a deep knowing that all was well, even though I was no longer in my body. I have no idea how long I was 'out of my body' because just as the binding laws of gravity did not hold any sway in this realm, neither did the laws of linear time. *I was free – totally free – free of all restrictions and limitations.*

Then, just as unexpectedly as I had found myself 'out of my body', I came back into it again. This time around, I was wide awake, staring up at the ceiling. My perspective had shifted 180 degrees from that free-floating state near the ceiling to being weighed down in the bed by the heaviness of my own body. I felt burdened not just physically but also emotionally, in stark contrast to the light state I had just experienced.

Although totally perplexed, I was aware that something profound had just occurred. As I had no rational way of explaining what had happened, I simply dismissed the experience. I reasoned with myself that it must have been a strange dream, a weird delusion or bizarre vision. I never tried to find out anything further about my experience or about 'out-of-body experiences' in general. Instead, I chose to block this episode from my mind. I did not fully recognise, until many years later, the significance of this turning point in my life.

In hindsight, I can see that this was my soul preparing me for what would come later in my life, by showing me an aspect of our existence of which I was not previously aware. The experience of leaving my body, albeit only to a few feet above me, to the ceiling of my bedroom, made it much easier for me to fully embrace my near death experience a decade later.

Over the next few days, I realised that I had to return to Ireland to stay. With the help of my friends, I came home in a wheelchair and was admitted to hospital. After weeks of tests, the doctors discovered that I had mononucleosis as well as a parasitic infection in my intestines, probably from the food poisoning in Mexico.

If I had stopped pushing myself to the point of exhaustion months earlier, I would have saved years of time recovering from those illnesses, and also what was later diagnosed as myalgic encephalomyelitis, more generally referred to as chronic fatigue syndrome (CFS).

I now know that everything happens for a reason. Sometimes, it is necessary to pass through what is often referred to as a 'dark night of the soul' to find out the true essence of who we really are.

CHAPTER 2

GIFT OF HEALTH

The next few months passed by in a blur. When I was discharged from the hospital, I moved back home and stayed with Mum and Dad, who were wonderfully caring.

My parents looked on anxiously as they saw me fading away in front of their eyes. I was barely able to eat and, as a consequence, lost a tremendous amount of weight. I will always remember the shocked expression on my friend Séamus's face, when he called in to see me on a short visit from London, about three months after I had returned home. As he stared at my tiny silhouette, he exclaimed, 'Róisín, you're only a shadow of your former self.'

By this time, I could hardly walk and I was often spending day after day and night after night bed-ridden in a darkened room. I felt like Gulliver, from Jonathan Swift's *Gulliver's Travels*, when he awoke in the land of Lilliput, washed ashore after a shipwreck and found himself tied down, restricted from moving by thousands of cords zigzagging across his entire body.[8] Similarly, I was barely able to move, bound by innumerable invisible threads. Though I was unaware of it at the time, these invisible threads were a gift from my soul. They formed a chrysalis, an outer casing, from which I would later emerge after I had reconnected with the beauty of my soul's true essence. But like any transition, I had to pass through the gooey, messy, viscous phase before any transformation could occur. This transition had to be extreme, as I had become so disconnected from my soul at this point in my life.

Exhaustion. Crushing, exhaustion. My sleeping pattern was so severely disrupted that I lost all sense of day and night as it meshed into one continuous haze. I developed a debilitating weakness in my arms and legs. In addition, a pain bored continuously, deep in the marrow of my bones as if it were draining my lifeblood.

My head ached relentlessly, alternating from a dull to a throbbing pain, especially when exposed to excessive light and brightness. Any chemical smells such as paint, perfume or aftershave were so toxic to my system that instantaneously upon sniffing them I would lose all my energy and become physically weak. I was freezing all the time. No matter how many layers I wore, the chill permeated to my core.

As the months passed, my condition deteriorated progressively. The doctors were perplexed by the ongoing disparity of my symptoms. They tested me for multiple sclerosis, cancer, Hodgkin's disease, tuberculosis and a whole battery of tropical diseases, but to no avail. Then, after six months, the medical consultant in charge of my case telephoned me at home. As I was mostly bed-bound at the time, I crawled on my hands and knees from my bed to reach the phone. I lay on the floor, with my ear on the receiver because I was physically unable to hold myself upright. Then I heard, 'Miss Fitzpatrick, all the test results are negative. We cannot find any illness other than the mononucleosis and giardiasis. They were diagnosed months ago and should be cleared by now. Since we cannot find any other illness, you must be healthy. I can no longer provide a medical certificate. You are ready to start working again in London.'

Like a boxer blindsided by an unexpected right hook, I lay there dazed, stunned by what I had just heard. How was I ever going to get dressed, take a plane to London and recommence working when my body was so incapacitated? Crying with sheer exasperation, I struggled to make it to the top of the stairs, and shuffled down, one step at a time, to reach my sister, who was at home. When I eventually reached her, I relayed what the doctor had said. I told her that I had to find another physician who would be willing to probe further and be able to assist me with finding a cure.

During this time period, I began to hear of an unusual illness called chronic fatigue syndrome. It was more of a catch-all, with the key symptom of total exhaustion to the point of being unable to live any kind of a normal life. I made an appointment to see the doctor who specialised in CFS in Dublin.

When I met with her, she immediately recognised my condition and diagnosed CFS. I was so grateful because a diagnosis had finally been made. Even though there were no known treatments then, she gave me invaluable advice, most notably to stop fighting the illness and to surrender to the fact that I was unwell. I had been wasting valuable energy which I could not afford to lose. I had to learn to relax and allow my body to recharge, as I was utterly depleted. I had to recognise this and learn to rebuild my strength slowly. She dealt with the medical administrative queries from my health insurance company, so that I could focus all my energy on regaining my health.

At this time, there was very little information available about CFS, and no consensus within the medical profession. Nonetheless, I tried to find any relevant literature in an attempt to gain my own understanding of this disease. I remember one day reading a book about CFS. The book included numerous case studies of patients with this illness, including a woman who described her life with CFS for the previous 25 years. At the time when I read this I was only 25 years old and became petrified by the prospect of being bed-ridden in a darkened room for all that time. It was inconceivable to me that the rest of my life would be spent trapped in my body instead of living life.

I realised that I was at the edge of a black void, staring into the abyss, about to embark on a long, dark, isolating, lonely journey into the unknown. There was no escape route. There was no way out. The only way to go was deep within. I had to face all my inner fears. And though at the time I certainly could not see this, being forced to stop, to become still and look within myself, was in fact one of the greatest blessings of my life.

I decided there and then that I would do everything within my limited power to regain as much of my health as possible, no matter how long it would take me. Irrespective of any failures *en route*, I had to reclaim my life. Although I was grateful to my parents for their unwavering support, I had always been self-reliant, so it was beyond frustrating as a mature adult to be dependent on them again. Even though it took years before I regained my health, it began that day, when I surrendered and followed my doctor's advice. By no longer wasting my energy battling the illness but embracing it, I began to move forward.

I was grateful that I was financially secure, with my medical insurance and disability payment from the European Bank. All of this, along with encouragement from my family and friends, made it possible for me to focus my limited energy resources on recovering my health. I felt fortunate that I was in such a position, as I knew others who were not as lucky and who had to struggle with both family and financial worries while trying to cope with this debilitating illness.

While searching for solutions, I attended a support group meeting for people with CFS. This organisation was set up with the objective of helping people with CFS to learn about the illness. At this meeting I met Conor and George, two men close to my age. The three of us talked and agreed that if we were going to get better, we would have to find a way ourselves. As there was no medical treatment available for CFS, we were willing to try natural medicine. We tried every herbal supplement and alternative diet we could find. Most importantly though, we decided to support each other along this journey. Although we never took any illicit or mind-altering drugs, we tasted some disgusting herbal concoctions out of sheer desperation to regain our health. If 'eye of newt' would have given us back our energy, we would have leapt at the opportunity!

During this time, I met another young person who lived near me, who also suffered from CFS. However, he had more of the cerebral symptoms of confusion and memory loss whereas I was physically weaker. We used to joke that if we could put his body together with my brain, at least one of us would be able to function properly!

One of my sisters visited every weekend. She would bring my duvet down onto the couch in the sunroom at the back of our parents' home. I would clamber onto the sofa and rest there for the afternoon. This provided a change of scenery for a little while. I really appreciated her kindness in spending so much time with me.

My friends were also wonderful and always stayed in touch throughout my illness. As the months and then the first year passed by, they never lost faith in my ability to heal. They visited me regularly on weekends and if I had the energy, they drove me to the pier at Howth Harbour, five minutes from my home but seemingly a world away when I was not able to leave the house on my own. I loved sitting on the wooden bench, listening to the soothing sounds of the sea swirling against the rocks and watching as the white spray spewed in all directions, creating a transparent haze reflecting miniature rainbows in the sunlight. I always felt more balanced by the sea. If I was exhausted, after a few moments of sitting near the shore I became more energised. Similarly, if I felt anxious or nervous, the sea would help me to feel calmer.

During this period of time there were many days when I was barely able to lift my arms or walk properly. I often had to heave myself onto the floor and crawl to get to the bathroom. There was still no recognised medical treatment or cure for CFS and all of the natural medicines that I had tried to date had been ineffective. Any glimmer of hope was quickly extinguished as the slightest improvement in my energy levels was only temporary. It was devastating to become overwhelmed again and again by the crippling fatigue. I was in my mid-twenties. I was not living. I was barely existing. The thought of having to endure this existence and remain this debilitated for the remainder of my life was terrifying.

As time passed, I became increasingly aware of the importance of keeping hope, and not letting it become totally extinguished. Hope for a cure. Hope for a better quality of life. Hope for making the best of this life. I knew that I had to maintain hope.

With this shared hope in mind, my family brought me to see *Riverdance*. I remember being so nervous not knowing if I would have enough energy to be able to go to the theatre, never mind sit through the performance. Thankfully, I managed on the night. Even though I was physically wiped out for days afterwards from the over-exertion, it was worth every minute because I came away feeling so inspired. Uplifted by the music and the choreography, it renewed my determination to make a recovery and to live a full life again.

A few months later, in yet another attempt to regain my health, I learned about a homeopathic practitioner living in my locality. I arranged an appointment to see her. My first visit to her clinic was the turning point on my path of recovery.

During the consultation she patiently listened to gain an understanding of my illness, and took copious notes before prescribing a homeopathic remedy. As I was leaving she gave me a book called *A Return to Love*, by Marianne Williamson. At this time, it was difficult for me to even hold my body upright in a sitting position and to lift my arm to turn the pages. Nonetheless, I knew that it was important, so I began to read this book as soon as I was back home.

In the text, which is a reflection on the principles of another book entitled *A Course in Miracles*, Marianne Williamson made reference to God and the Holy Spirit. Although I was raised Catholic, I did not believe in any sort of religious or spiritual practice at this point in my life. I fully respected that faith could be fulfilling for other people if it gave some strength to overcome life's challenges, but faith was not for me.

Despite my reservations, this book turned my life around. Williamson's book described God in the most simple yet potent of terms: *love*.[9] She proposed that when we embrace this love in our lives, we create the opportunity for our inner light to shine because we connect with who we are truly meant to be. *For the first time, I realised that we are all pure love, we just have to let go of our fears and negative beliefs for our souls' truths to be expressed.*

Although at the time still an atheist, I started to open my mind to the possibility of a Divine presence. Ironically, I could not feel it in my heart, but intellectually I began to see that there might be more to living than I had previously been willing to consider. A small chink appeared in the armour that I had built around my life. Through this tiny crack, I caught a glimmer of light.

A huge part of me did not want to see this, as it would be so overwhelming to open up to the possibility of this truth. It would mean questioning all aspects of my life, from who I am, to why I exist. Until then my way of understanding was to comprehend an idea rationally before I could believe. If I opened up, this would require believing before I could rationally understand.

A few months later, I decided to see a spiritual healer. Although I was initially sceptical of the idea, after groping in the dark for such a long period of time, I was so desperate to recover my health that I was willing to try *anything* that might potentially increase my energy. I opened up to the possibility that spiritual healing might be of assistance and made an appointment to see a healer who had an excellent reputation. The ensuing session was truly remarkable.

As she placed her hands close to my body I began to feel a sensation of pins and needles. Wherever she held her hands, over my stomach, legs or head, I felt this tingling sensation increasing in strength. As the session continued, the feeling became stronger and stronger until it suddenly transformed into powerful surges of energy that pulsated throughout my entire being. With these waves of energy, my limbs became lighter as my body came to life once again.

Similar to Gulliver, after he had found an inner strength to tear away the zigzagged ropes that bound him, I regained the strength to unfasten the invisible cords which had surrounded me for the previous couple of years.

After the physical but most especially the spiritual awakening, I understood for the first time that we are all part of something grander, a larger existence in this universe. I realised the presence of a Source of power beyond the vision of our naked eyes and limited awareness of our physical senses, something I would later come to call Universal Consciousness.

After this experience, I developed a radically different way of perceiving life and being in the world. It meant giving up intellectual control and surrendering to an unfathomable and intangible Power. On one hand, this was an amazing realisation. On the other, it was very frightening, as it forced me to see a much bigger part of my life which was beyond my control.

The chink in the armour of my life cracked wide open, allowing me to embrace my heart as well as my head. I was now able to feel this life-force. Although I could not explain it, or fully comprehend it, I knew that it existed and that I was part of this field of energy, as is everyone. The only way that I was able to make some sense of this whole experience was to look at the stars, the beauty of nature, the seas and the mountains and to ask: what energy created these?

Ironically, I was looking for physical energy but ultimately, I was given the much greater gift of reconnecting with the energy of my soul.

Finally, I began to regain my energy little by little, and, most importantly, to maintain the improvement. Having been so debilitated for the previous couple of years, this was the first time that I managed to sustain some steady progress towards the recovery of my health.

As my spiritual awareness expanded, I began studying natural medicine and homeopathy. This was when I understood the underlying cause of my CFS illness. For years I had been trying to identify a specific disease and treat it, when in reality, my illness was caused by my body being run-down by extreme stress and strain. Over time, I had compromised my immune system and become susceptible to viruses and infections, which in turn weakened my immune system even further.

At a much deeper level, I believe that the root cause of my illness was rejection of living my soul's truth. I was able to see that the physical illness was a manifestation of the degree to which I had disconnected from my soul.

I realised that instead of taking the approach of attacking the disease, what I really needed to do was to nurture my body and soul to create health from within.

As I took better care of my body, mind and spirit through natural medicine, meditation, eating healthy food and practising some gentle yoga moves, I gradually restored my health. As I reconnected with the energy of my soul, I became healthier with every week, month and year that passed.

I was grateful that the European Bank had kept my position open for me throughout the period of my illness. However, I realised that I would not be able to return to the bank, as my previous professional life was no longer aligned with my soul's path. Giving up this security was a huge step at the time because I had not fully regained my health.

I also knew that I would have to find my own way in life, and that my university degrees, diplomas and languages were useless now. Who would ever hire anyone who had been ill for so long? I had learned the skill of how to crawl on my hands and knees for the previous few years. This had given me a whole new perspective on life, from the ground up, but it certainly was not going to help with answering that daft question in a job interview, 'Where do you see yourself in five years' time?' Hopefully walking upright, that would be a start!

Nonetheless, I knew that if I had the courage to take the leap of faith, this Divine form of wisdom would respond by opening up new, unforeseen opportunities.

Though challenging at the time, I summoned all my courage and took the leap.

My health continued to improve slowly as I continued to study, and finally complete my four-year qualification in homeopathy. Understanding the power of realigning with my deepest truth – mentally, emotionally and physically – was like tuning a musical instrument. When everything was in sync again, my life-force flowed beautifully. My energy levels increased. I felt alive and I was able to pick up the pieces of my life and start living again.

While on holiday in the west of Ireland, I took a sailing course for a week. After the long period of illness of barely being able to sit by the shore, it was a joy to experience the feeling of freedom gliding over the waves. During that holiday I also swam in the sea and loved being in the water; rough or calm, it didn't matter. Whether tossed by the crashing waves or floating on the smooth surface of the ocean, to this day I always find the sea to be a wonderful teacher of life: how to take risks, dive in, or simply go with the flow.

Over that week's holiday, I made some new friends, one of whom introduced me to salsa dancing. The rest, as they say, is history. Once I was strong enough, I began to go out to meet friends and to dance a little. I became part of a fun-loving and positive group of people. We all enjoyed being given a second chance at our twenties, even though we were in our thirties, with everyone encouraging the best in each other both on and off the dance floor.

When I was dancing, I was on cloud nine, spinning and turning around the dance floor at rapid speed.

Everyone always said that I looked so happy. It did not matter to me if my dance partner or I totally messed up a move, I would still have a huge smile on my face. Every time my dance partner did a dip or turn or something went wrong, and I ended up on the floor or in some twisted contortion that even Houdini couldn't escape, I did not care. We would laugh and just keep dancing. The inspiration from *Riverdance* had become a reality. I was dancing to the tune of life.

Upon waking in the mornings, instead of thinking about illness and how to find a cure, a salsa melody played in my head and I felt light and joyous. By constantly listening and dancing to the music, I had changed the thoughts in my mind. To this day, if I am stressed or worried about anything, I put on my dancing shoes and change the tune that I choose to dance my life to, in every sense of the word.

When I had almost fully regained my health, I bought a beautiful home, approximately 30 minutes' drive from Dublin city centre. This home provided a safe place to complete my healing from CFS. It nourishes my soul because it is situated a stone's throw from the sea. The open water centres me in my deepest truth. I feel my spirits lifted in times of trouble, or at peace in times of strife.

CFS was a real blessing, although it was incredibly well disguised at the time. I joke that I had my mid-life crisis early – at the age of 25! Even if I could turn the clocks back, I would not change one single moment of the whole experience. I learned that there is a Greater Power that is all around us, and also comes through us if we choose to align with this Divine form of wisdom. And, once this has been accessed, it always remains with us as a sacred gift.

Prior to the CFS, I would not have been a big believer in 'miracles' – or at least, I would have questioned what a miracle was or could be in my life. It felt, though, truly miraculous to be gradually returning to a functioning body. The invisible cords which had formed a cocoon around me turned out to be a gift from my soul. Like a butterfly emerging from the chrysalis, I left the sheath behind as I slowly unfurled my wings. This physical and spiritual metamorphosis was a painful and often muddled process but ultimately a beautiful one, as I gained my freedom to live a more empowered life. In a relatively short period of time, I had gone from being a healthy young woman in my twenties, performing high-level international relations work, to being so physically incapacitated that on really bad days, there were times when I could only move my eyeballs. As my energy came back, it was as if God – Divine Source of energy, Greater Power, or Universal Consciousness, whatever terminology you wish to use – were breathing new life into this lifeless body. With each breath came a whole new appreciation of living.

I knew when I had overcome CFS that I would be able to cope with anything. I learned that as long as my mind was able to function, I could make choices and intentionally choose to connect with the power of this Divine form of wisdom and be guided. I also knew that once my body worked fully again, I would physically be able to remove myself from any situation that was not my soul's truth. I would be able to overcome any financial situation, relationship issues, or emotional crisis.

After I qualified as a homeopath, I set up my own practice. I had always wished to help to create – in some way, shape or form – a better world. In my early twenties, I focused my positive intention towards the world through my work in international relations. Now, homeopathy provided a new path and new insights, as part of the same journey, with the same intention. I observed in my practice that it was those clients who took full responsibility for their lives and consciously made changes who could achieve astounding results. I was inspired by their courage, as they created their lives anew. However, those who did not choose to take responsibility tended to remain stuck in the same patterns. Observing these dynamics provided a huge learning experience, confirming the power of this Divine form of wisdom and how each one of us has equal access to this Source of energy. The only difference is whether we make the decision to live from the limited perspective of this physical world, or have enough faith to trust in the invisible but unlimited Power of Universal Consciousness.

Prior to being ill with CFS, I used to identify myself through my job, as opposed to who I was as a person. This was due in part to learned behaviour from society, but at a deeper level I did not really know who I was at the time. For years, over-working had been an effective but ultimately self-destructive way of not facing my inner fears and unhappiness. In certain ways, it is an addiction that society encourages, which has a short-term double benefit of avoiding the deeper issues within *and* receiving praise for avoiding them!

Conor, whom I met at the CFS support group, always used to say when we were going through the hell of CFS that he would not have wished it on his worst enemy. Now, having come through to the other side, he says that he would wish it for his best friend. I know this sounds strange, but it is true. During the process of recovering from CFS, I learned that I had to reconnect with my emotions and allow myself to feel the depth of the pain of being isolated by the illness. I also gained an understanding of why I had chosen to over-work in the first place. By being forced to stop, go within, face all my inner fears and look at them head on, I have come to fully appreciate that only love is real. The rest is an illusion.

Life is so hectic and fast-paced that we seldom get the chance to go deep within and find out who we truly are, and discover our purpose. Had I not been stopped in my tracks, there is no way that I would ever have gone there of my own volition. I believe that Universal Consciousness gives us opportunities – whether in the form of illness, financial crises, bereavement or other challenges – to wake up from the illusion of this so-called 'reality' and to see the true meaning of life. This Divine form of wisdom gently whispers in our ear and becomes louder and louder until we listen.

Over the years, I have learned to allow this Divine form of wisdom to show me the way forward, as it has the full view of all possibilities and potential for my soul. Challenging though it may be, trusting in the wisdom of this Universal Consciousness *always* proves to be the best path, even if I cannot fully understand it at the time. Intellectually, my head may be focused in one direction, but deep in my heart I hear that faint yet persistent calling and I now listen quietly to this guidance from within.

With a whole new appreciation of life, I also gained a much greater respect for my body. I had always taken my health for granted and from this experience I learned to take care of myself, body and soul. They say that if you overcome a serious illness early in life, you then go on to lead a long, healthy and happy life. This is so true. When we do not appreciate our health, we tend to abuse our bodies, for instance by drinking too much caffeine or eating processed food (where there can be more nutrition in the wrapping than in the so-called food). However, we still expect our bodies to work perfectly. We maintain our houses, our cars and even our gas boilers, but our bodies – which are the dwelling places for our souls – we abuse.

Instead of trying to suppress physical symptoms if they appear, I have learned to stop and listen, knowing that my soul is trying to get my attention by giving me a sign that I need to readjust my path in life. By focusing on prevention as the best cure, rather than quickly taking medicines for minor symptoms as they appear, I search for the deeper meaning and root cause of the 'dis-ease'. For example, if I get an ache or pain in my body,

I choose to become still, and place my awareness on the symptoms. Often I experience insights as to why I have the symptom and am always grateful for the messages. When I then make the necessary adjustments in my life and, as the emotional or mental 'dis-ease' is sorted, the physical symptoms are usually alleviated.

Looking back, I believe that this Divine form of wisdom was always guiding me. It knew how to communicate with me in a way that I would be able to hear. Initially, because I stubbornly refused to pay attention, I was brought to my knees. Then, I realised that the illness had provided an opportunity to reconnect with my soul's truth. The road to recovery from CFS was truly a healing path. It was not just a way of reclaiming my health from CFS; it was much more importantly a journey to embrace my soul and the infinite power of Universal Consciousness. This was a huge gift from that period of my life.

One Saturday evening in March 2004, I celebrated my birthday with some friends from my salsa dancing group. Life was amazing once again. I had regained my health and vitality – so much so that I did not feel the need to think twice about my energy levels or about the strength of my immune system. During dinner I spoke with Lisa, one of my close pals. I was elated because I had finally made a full recovery from CFS: the nightmare was over. I was totally free, feeling vibrant and filled with enthusiasm for life once again. It was a joyful evening, and we danced until the sun came up, with the dawning of a new chapter in my life.

Later that day, I drove to Loughcrew, the location of one of the ancient megalithic (*mega*, large; *lithos*, stone) sites in Ireland. I love visiting this sacred place because it is where I can become still and quietly connect with my soul. When I was there, I focused on how grateful I was for regaining my health and life once again. Over the previous week, knowing that I was about to embark on a new phase in my life, I had chosen to fully live life by experiencing my soul's loving light and to share it with others. When I was at Loughrew on that Sunday, I reaffirmed my intention by making a request to become 'a clear channel for the light', however, I forgot to mention the words, 'Gently, please!'

CHAPTER 3

GIFT OF THE LIGHT: MY NEAR-DEATH EXPERIENCE

When I set the intention to incorporate this loving light into my life, my request was heard and answered the following day, but in a way that I could never have predicted.

In the early afternoon of Monday 22 March 2004, without any warning, a sharp pain shot through the base of my neck and ricocheted throughout my skull. My head wrenched backwards in excruciating agony, pulled by a severe spasm. This pain was like nothing I had ever experienced before.

I was at home that day, quietly sitting in my bedroom listening to some music while enjoying a leisurely day off from work. Then in one instant, as I stood up and turned my head to leave the room, everything shifted from calm

to chaos. A shrill pain suddenly roared through my head
like a hurricane, as my whole life began to spin out of
control. This pain rendered me powerless in its wake.

I thought that if I could just lie down and breathe
slowly, then surely it would relieve the pain. I tried
lying completely motionless on my bed, hoping that
the stillness would provide some relief, even if only
momentary. But it was no use. If anything, the intensity
of the pain increased, as it whipped up into and then
through my head. At this point, I began to feel waves
of nausea. I scrambled to the bathroom and instantly
began vomiting, as hot and cold sweats coursed through
my body. The spasms in my neck arched my head
backwards, making vomiting unbearably painful each
time my head lunged forward. I also became extremely
light-headed, and grew weaker each time I vomited. I
knew that I could pass out at any moment.

From the medical training I had received while
studying homeopathy, I knew how to recognise the
symptoms of a brain haemorrhage. The thought flashed
through the whirling chaos in my mind: *brain haemorrhage,
Róisín, you are having a brain haemorrhage*. I knew that time
would be of the essence. As I was alone in my home, I used
what little strength I had to call an ambulance.

'Please help me. I need assistance urgently. I've a
dreadful pain in my head and am scared that I will lose
consciousness. Can you send an ambulance as quickly
as you can?' After giving the address and directions for
my house to the operator, I hung up the phone. Clinging
to the banister, I made my way down the stairs, terrified

that I would pass out before I could reach the entrance of my home. Relieved when I made it to the front door, I waited for the emergency services to arrive. I realised that my life had been turned upside down in an instant. Even though I was in agonising pain, I chose to try to remain calm while waiting for the ambulance, hoping that it would increase my chances of pulling through this crisis.

Standing at the door, I watched helplessly as the ambulance sped past my home. I waved my arms in the air, trying to attract their attention, but I could no longer hold myself upright. I collapsed on my knees. Fortunately, at that moment the paramedic saw me and immediately shouted at the driver to reverse. He ran towards my house and into the front hallway. Kevin, the paramedic, then asked me several questions as he tried to assess my condition. I was still able to speak clearly at this stage and could articulate words to relay the symptoms.

They brought me out to the ambulance and strapped me onto the stretcher. I remember thinking to myself: why is this happening? Was the intention I had set the previous day at Loughcrew for connecting with the powerful love of Universal Consciousness being answered? If this was the case, this certainly was *not* what I'd anticipated. In my naiveté, I had expected a joyful contemplative experience, one of those great meditations where every worry in the world dissolves, where time is suspended, and life becomes a peaceful, wondrous journey.

Instead, I found myself on the flat of my back once again and in a critical condition, in the back of an ambulance on my way to the hospital. I thought, you have got to be kidding me!

As we drove away, Kevin continued to speak with me, making sure I remained conscious. He was also trying to determine whether the symptoms were of a brain haemorrhage or meningitis. Given the sudden onset, a cerebral haemorrhage was more likely to have been the cause.

Due to the significant risk of a haemorrhage, the ambulance driver proceeded slowly, in order to avoid any bumps in the road, which could in turn have increased the leakage of blood into my brain. Even though he took this precaution, I could still feel the uneven terrain of the road surface below me, as each bump reverberated through my head. In the background, I could hear the din of the screaming siren as we made our way to the hospital through the streets and on to the motorway heading towards St Columcille's Hospital in Loughlinstown. When we arrived at the hospital about 15 minutes later, the accident and emergency unit (A&E) was teeming with patients. I was still vomiting, and in tears from the pain in my head and neck. The hospital was short-staffed and the nurses were overwhelmed by the number of patients. They asked Kevin if he could leave me in a chair. I remember looking up at him in disbelief, as my neck was so weak that it would have been impossible for me to hold myself upright.

Kevin was fully aware of my condition; he stood by

my stretcher and told me that he would stay there until I was given a hospital trolley. He made a call to ambulance control to let them know about the situation.

After a while, I was eventually placed on a hospital trolley and moved to a side room. I began to feel hypersensitivity in all my senses. The blinding florescent light directly above my head seemed to bore into my eyes. The noise and commotion of the A&E unit clattered in my ears with the crashing and clanging sounds of metal on metal from the movement of the hospital trollies. The chemical odours from the cleaning agents were suffocating and made me feel even more nauseous. Despite this increasing sensitivity, I tried to remain calm.

When the doctor came to examine me she immediately recognised the severity of my symptoms. After taking a detailed case history and performing a clinical examination, she took some blood tests and organised a brain scan (computerised tomography of the brain).[10] A short while later, she told me that I was indeed having a brain haemorrhage and that they would have to transfer me to the neurosurgical unit at Beaumont Hospital, (the Irish centre for excellence in neurosurgery), about 45 minutes away by ambulance.

When my parents arrived, I remember using all my energy trying to make light of the situation. Mum told me afterwards that she knew I was going to be fine because I had been laughing with them. She had no idea that by this time, it was becoming extremely difficult for me to put words together to construct sentences. It was like trying to assemble a jigsaw puzzle. Although

I didn't let on to my parents, I was terrified, as I knew that this was another part of my brain function that was gradually slipping away.

Later in the evening I was transferred into another ambulance, which brought me to Beaumont hospital. It was necessary to have a specialist nurse to accompany me in the ambulance because of the potential risks associated with my condition. Similar to the ambulance ride earlier that day, the driver drove slowly to ensure that the trip was as smooth as possible. With the siren whirring overhead, I lay there transfixed as I watched the faint glow of the blue light spinning around and around through the glass. I tried to stay centred and calm throughout the journey.

When I arrived at the brain trauma unit at Beaumont Hospital, the doctor told me, 'With a brain haemorrhage there is a high risk of dying, or of having a stroke which could cause paralysis. You will need to have an angiogram in the morning to investigate the source and size of the haemorrhage in your brain. Depending on the results, you may need to have an operation to stop the bleeding and reduce the pressure of fluid on your brain.' When I asked her what the potential complications might be, she continued to explain, 'Paralysis, loss of sight or memory dysfunction.'[11]

I was aware that this whole incident was exhausting for my mother as she heard this news about the potential risks to her youngest daughter's life. I encouraged my parents to go home so that Mum could rest. The hospital environment was far too challenging for her, and there was nothing that either of them could do for me in any case. After they left, I was admitted to the intensive care unit (ICU).

In the ICU, the enormity of my situation became clear to me. I had managed to remain calm for most of the day; this was the first time that fear overwhelmed me. The tears I had shed previously were due to the severity of the pain that I had been enduring. Now, in addition to the physical pain pummelling in my head, my tears were also of deep raw emotion as I faced this challenging situation.

I called for the nurse, and a gentle-natured woman came over to me. I asked her to be honest, as I wanted to know the truth. As I asked her questions about brain haemorrhages and medical procedures, she smiled as she tried to reassure me. Holding my hand and looking straight into my eyes, she answered my queries and kindly stayed with me for a while to help me to cope with all that was happening.

After she left, I lay there, one of six people in the ICU, knowing that I had the choice to allow myself to get caught up and buffeted by the hurricane whirling around in my head, or to centre myself and remain calm in the eye of the storm. I had the choice to go into the fear of death, fear of being paralysed, and fear of the potential risks associated with brain surgery. The alternative choice was to try to remain as calm as possible, by focusing my attention on being in the moment, hoping that this might help me.

Every time any thoughts of fear, death, paralysis or being disabled came to mind, I chose to let those thoughts pass, as I maintained steady concentration on breathing slowly. It was difficult to keep my focus on being in the moment because of the severity of my physical symptoms. The pain pounded relentlessly in my head. This was accompanied by waves of hot and cold sweats surging throughout my body while my stomach churned with nausea. Despite these conditions, I persisted.

Although I was in charge of making the decision to be in the moment, what happened next was totally unforeseen, and completely out of my control. All I could do was surrender to the experience.*

WHOOOOOOOSH ... as I suddenly found myself drawn out of my body ... *I feel amazing! Floating, weightless ... what is this sense of freedom, this boundless freedom?* Then I glimpsed a light, a shimmering light, as if peering through the haze of sunlight on a scorching hot day. The brilliant light refracted everywhere into tiny glistening sparks of ignited energy – beautiful, bright, breathtaking.

Pulled by this light, I let go totally. I surrendered as a profound peace and gentle exuberance began to radiate throughout my whole being. Suddenly it dawned on me that the agonising pain had vanished, and I thought to myself: 'why am I no longer feeling the pounding

---

* Note to reader: I endeavour to share the beauty of this experience in a way that you can hopefully feel it for yourself. This is challenging because we have not developed the language for describing this boundless, unconditional love and eternal light. We have extensive vernacular to describe war, hatred, violence and greed in minute detail, but for love, infinite love, the ultimate Source from which we are all created and the reason why we continue to live after we 'die', we simply don't have the words! What I am lacking in vocabulary, I hope to make up for in passion so that you can experience this journey with me. I invite you to open your mind to the possibility that it is not necessary to have an NDE to be able to tap into the truth of who you really are. All that is required is a willingness on your part to have a wider vision to see that there might be more to life than is visible to our eyes. To quote the veracious advice of Antoine de Saint-Exupéry's *The Little Prince*, 'One sees clearly only with the heart. What is essential is invisible to the eyes.'

pain from the haemorrhage? I'm not feeling any pain whatsoever. Why am I no longer frightened? I'm not at all fearful or anxious.' I felt totally free. As I continued to relinquish all resistance, I allowed this crystalline light to permeate through me and to surround me.

With full 360-degree panoramic vision I was able to see all around me. Everywhere I looked, I was encircled by flickering, iridescent lights. They reminded me of fireflies, but not 20 or 30, as one might be lucky enough to see on a balmy summer's night. There were myriads, more than hundreds, thousands, millions or even billions. Struck by the sheer magnificence of this scene, I watched the immeasurable number of lights glow, extending on and on and on as all these minuscule sparks of light merged to create one unified expanse. This light seemed to blaze into eternity.

Radiating all around, above, below, in front, behind and stretching for as far as I could see, the light warmly enveloped me. With no weight or density, 'I' was now becoming part of this dynamic and intensely powerful energy. Mesmerised, I realised that 'I' still existed, but *who am I? What am I?* I had always associated myself with my body but I was not in my body anymore. I became aware of being part of a much grander existence, greater than anything I had ever consciously lived before.

It is nearly impossible to convey this experience in words, but try for a moment to imagine being a tiny speck of snow in a recently shaken Christmas snow-globe. Surrounded, you find yourself amidst a flurry of thousands of crystalline snowflakes, swirling and spinning in a surreal slow-motion. The light refracts off each tiny flake, transforming something ordinary into a magical and extraordinary experience.

Now imagine that you are no longer encased in the glass sphere. Instead, this glistening light extends as far as your eyes can see and then beyond. In this dimension, the laws of time and gravity do not exist. The whirling motion continues. Transfixed by the frenzied but trance-like commotion, you are suspended as part of a timeless continuum within this immeasurable space. This existence naturally flows and overflows to infinity as you feel yourself surrounded by this beautiful, all-encompassing, radiant light.

As my journey continued, I became captivated by the magnificence of the light. I saw it morph from an infinite number of individual speckles, into undulating waves of light and pure love. Slowly, as if suspended in time, the waves gently oscillated, surging to form a crest and then softly subsiding. These waves continued in an endless flow.

Gradually, the white light transformed into an opalescent hue, as the speckles of light, now flowing as waves, refracted an array of vivid colours. The rolling waves, golden in colour (tinged with salmon-pink, tangerine-orange and lavender) ascended and descended as they continuously merged with each other.

The closest comparison to this in the physical world would be the sensation of flying and looking down on the clouds, when the sun is setting or rising – seeing an infinite horizon of luminescent waves. However, unlike clouds, which appear static, in this vast unending expanse the energy is vibrant, alive, and ebullient with dynamic potential. This energy feels like it is bursting with possibilities.

Try to imagine not only that you *see* these waves of light, but also that you *become part of* them. In this way, rather than seeing yourself as existing above the waves, allow yourself to integrate with this energy field of pure love, so that you can feel yourself being embraced by boundless bliss.

Finally, after a lifetime of searching, I find the true meaning of love. Incomprehensible in our daily 'reality' in the physical world, yet so natural and all-pervasive in this realm, this euphoric love is all that exists. This is who I am. It is my deepest truth. This is the deepest truth of each and every one of us: *we are pure love – a love that is so indescribable, unfathomable yet real, pure and blissful, oh so blissful ...*

Enveloped by the warmth of this vast existence, the colours evolved once again. I watched, entranced by the extraordinary intensity of the colours as they flashed through like the aurora borealis. Powerful sheets of light energy illuminated the entire space, one following the other in a stunning display of violet, then crimson red, followed by magenta, superseded by verdant green, and then by azure, replaced in turn by a glowing, fire-like amber. The spectacle continued as each of the colours emitted its own beautiful, lustrous light.

Then patterns started to emerge, as a countless number of fantastic designs twirled like eddies, spiralling and turning, alternating in a continuous procession, as one surreal image followed another and another, all brilliantly out-marvelling its predecessor. The phenomenal energy and prismatic colours exploded with vitality – erupting, gushing and spewing in all directions. Throughout this visual display of innumerable variations of light, the most significant and persistent sensation was of palpable love as a constant presence.

Even more significantly, the light and the overwhelming sense of a present love all around me was not accompanied by any sound. None at all. Although the colours and waves of light were pulsating with energy, I was paradoxically surrounded by a hushed silence. Immersed in a deep inner peace, I became infused with a serene stillness, a tranquillity that transcended everything: a knowing that all was perfect.

I stayed there, dwelling in this vibration – I have no idea for how long. There was no sense of linear time or spatial limitations as I was beyond the physical realm. In this limitless expanse of oneness I was fully aware that I was experiencing the Source from which we all originate.

I felt a profound sense of belonging, and a deep knowing that this is our core truth. *We are pure energy. We are pure love.*

From the moment I entered this Higher Realm, I surrendered to and trusted the entire experience. As the journey progressed, I came to realise that I am, as everyone is, part of an infinite universe, so immense in scale that we could never fully comprehend its size within the constraints of our limited minds.

I understood that life is truly everlasting. It is an

unending stream of consciousness. We continue to exist after our life-force leaves our bodies. Our true essence is eternal. I was aware that if it was my time to 'die', I would willingly choose to go. Indeed, the bliss I experienced of the ecstatic love was so enticing ... so incredibly enthralling ... that I found it extremely difficult to make the decision to come back. If my parents had not been alive at the time, I would have chosen to stay in the infinite. I would not have come back.

However, I knew that the emotional shock would have been too difficult for my parents, most especially for my mother. She had always said that it was her greatest fear to bury one of her children. I simply could not do this to her. I also wanted to remain with my parents in order to care for them as they grew older, just as they had been there for me when I was ill in my twenties.

While out of my body, I had been brought beyond the physical pain and environment of the ICU. Out of my body, calmness and alertness and awareness felt easy, even effortless. I remember thinking to myself: *how am I going to fit all of this boundless energy of love and light back into my body? How would I ever compress infinity back into such a minuscule and restrictive physical form?*

I have to come back. I have to return. Unbearable as it was for me to separate myself from this loving state, I made the decision to go back to my body.

Once I had made the decision to return from this ecstatic realm, I came back in an instant. The swooping descent from soaring in the sublime back down to earth was sudden: Crash! Bang! Wallop!

The reality of my return to embodiment was so abrupt it was almost comic, and it involved Paddy, an elderly gentleman in the bed across from mine in the ICU. He was obviously suffering, as the stream of obscenities he shouted consisted of an extensive vocabulary of a four-letter word beginning with 'F*' followed by 'OFF!' This was repeated mechanically like rounds from a machine gun. 'F*** OFF, F*** OFF, F*** OFF!' Paddy's solo cacophony told me that I was back on earth for sure, and in hospital. I found myself in my body, facing all the physical pain and fear associated with a brain haemorrhage once again. This hard knock struck me instantly, in stark contrast to the feeling of bliss I had just experienced as part of the oneness of Universal Consciousness.

I chose to keep my focus on the present moment. Then, beyond my control, WHOOOOOOOSH … I was drawn out of my body for a second time. As I became part of the oneness again, I surrendered and merged with the vast expanse. A feeling of tranquil peace surrounded and imbued my very essence. I remember being stunned by the revelation that 'I' still existed, even though I was out of my body once again. This experience was as powerful as it had been the first time. I realised that the physical suit of skin and bone with which I had always identified myself was actually irrelevant, now that I was no longer in my body.

It was amazing to discover that consciousness is much greater than the purely physical constituents of body or brain.

I thought: 'how can I exist as a separate entity from

my body? How can I still exist even though I am not in a physical form? If I am not my body then who am I? What is life? What does being alive really mean? What is death? Who is doing the thinking?' I had always thought that consciousness was connected to embodiment. What else could I have known? Every question that I asked was answered instantaneously. The oneness permeated my being, so that as soon as I asked a question, I simultaneously received an answer. Answers came to me not in words, but rather in the certainty of having been imparted with knowledge: I simply 'knew' the answers. Irrespective of the question, the answer was always the same – love. The all-pervasive love, profound love, peaceful love, pure love, infused my very essence. As if by osmosis, I absorbed the answer when I was immersed in the waves of this Universal Consciousness.

Then: "F*** OFF, F*** OFF, F*** OFF!" Paddy's diatribe reverberated throughout the ICU and I landed with a bang back in my body once again. There was chaos and commotion as the nurses tried to relieve Paddy's distress. While they were calmly trying to comfort him, I was reeling between realism and surrealism. Landing back in my body was a horrendous shock. It was such a difficult transition from the never-ending stillness and serenity. I was writhing in pain from the severity of the headache, yet I believed that if I tried to move it could have devastating consequences. I lay there faced with the dilemma of choice between the austere experience of being in a seriously ill human body, or the immeasurable freedom and peace of spirit of being part of Universal Consciousness.

At this time, I decided to deliberately face the fear of
having a stroke. The doctor had said that I risked being
paralysed for the rest of my life. I had already been in a
bed-bound situation in my twenties with CFS, so I knew
all too well what that would entail. I imagined what it
would be like to be in a body paralysed by a stroke –
unable to walk, dance, or do anything independently.
I chose to be fully present in the moment, and once
again, WHOOOOOOOSH … I suddenly found myself
brought out into the immeasurable expanse. I connected
with and became one with this phenomenal energy. I
reconfirmed that 'I' still existed, but as part of something
much greater than I had ever previously conceptualised.
The vast expanse of unbounded bliss was more real than
anything I had ever experienced in the years prior to
that point in my life. I was in this state of timelessness,
so I had no idea how long I was there.

Then, yet again, I was hurtled back into my body. This
time when I returned, I was still able to maintain the
connection to this extraordinary life-force. I could feel
the light joyfulness of ecstatic loving energy pulsating
throughout my body. I knew that even in the worst-
case scenario of having a stroke and being paralysed,
this beautiful sense of union would always be with me,
helping me to cope.

I realised from that moment on that I could always
access this state of being. I then began to feel and
experience this amazing energy in my body, and
imagined it pulsing through me and helping me to live a
full and dynamic life. I saw myself first as spinning and

turning on the dance floor, then as walking in nature and having total physical freedom in my body. By choosing to focus all my attention on integrating completely with this energy and making a full recovery, I experienced vibrating waves of blissful energy swirling around my body. After becoming one with the pure love of Universal Consciousness, I realised that everything was possible.

During this cascading series of sequences in which I was repeatedly drawn out of my body, I became one with unconditional love and serene peace, over and over and over again. Each time I was able to bring this energy back as I returned to my physical body. This process continued throughout the remainder of the night as this heightened state of being stayed with me.

The following morning, a hospital porter wheeled me into the radiology department for an angiogram in order for the doctors to see the location and size of the brain haemorrhage on an X-ray, to determine if I required surgery. I remember trying to joke with the doctor, saying, 'I hope you find a brain in there.' He smiled, as he knew that I was nervous and that this was my way of releasing tension.

The doctor stared at the screen for what seemed like an eternity. He kept staring and staring at the image. By this time I was beginning to get anxious, because he said absolutely nothing.

Finally, he turned and looked at me as he said, 'You're one lucky lady. Although you have had a brain haemorrhage, the good news is that the bleeding appears to have stopped of its own accord and the swelling has subsided. It is not necessary for us to perform an operation to relieve the pressure of fluid on your brain.'[12]

A few tears trickled down the side of my face onto the sheet below me as I let out a huge sigh, and exhaled with sheer relief. In the ICU, I had held my emotions in check while I focused on being in the moment and not relinquishing my power to fear. Now, deep within, I knew that I would make a full recovery. Through connecting with the blissful energy of my NDE, I would be able to live a more empowered life from thereon.

Over the next few days I had more powerful healing experiences that affected me profoundly. The strongest of these occurred during the following day and evening. These post-NDE experiences were very much a part of the whole process, as everything merged in this timeless continuum. These were not dreams, because dreams have a vague, illusory and distorted feeling. By contrast, these experiences were more like visions because they were sharp, clear and focused.[13]

The first experience was a vision of being held in the palm of God's hand. This enormous yet benevolent hand was strong and stable, as it supported me while I lay curled up in the foetal position. In many ways, I was like a new-born, vulnerable and delicate. I felt safe, embedded in the soft creases of His warm hand, protected in every way. I kept hearing the words, 'Surrender to the bliss' over and over again as they repeated in my head. As I heard the words, that is exactly what I chose to do, moment by moment. I surrendered to the experience. They were spoken as a gentle command, entreating me to accept all the tenderness of this loving compassion. My role was to trust, simply let go and allow my body to heal during the recovery process. At this time in my life, I had completely forgotten the beautiful Irish blessing for wishing safe travels, 'May the road rise up to meet you', which ends with the phrase '... and until we meet again, may God hold you in the palm of His hand.'[15]

It was only many years later, when I visited a friend's home in Connecticut for Thanksgiving, that I happened to see this blessing hanging in a picture frame just inside her front door, 'May God hold you in the palm of His hand.' Those words reminded me instantly of the feeling which is indelibly etched in my heart from when I was in the ICU. At the time, I knew that I was embarking on not only a physical journey, but more importantly a spiritual one to reconnect with my soul. I realised that I was completely safe because I was accompanied by a Divine presence which supported and encouraged me all the way.[16] God held me in the palm of His hand during that extraordinary time in my life, as He is still holding me, guiding me through my life now.

The second strong vision was of disembarking from a huge, black ship, which ominously blocked out the skyline behind me. In front of me lay a short wooden pier. As I strode to the end of this pier, I found myself surrounded by a crystal-clear, turquoise, sparkling ocean. The water shimmered with light and vibrancy. I dove in and went down, down, down ... there was no end and the colour of the sea remained just as brilliant as it was on the surface. Then I floated up, up, up ... into the eternity of the azure sky, again there was no end as the sky maintained its beautifully rich cerulean hue. These were the depths and the heights of this paradise. I realised that they represented how, if I could leave my fears behind, the bliss I experienced during my NDE could be recreated here on earth by keeping my heart and mind open to this infinite Source of energy.

The third visionary experience was of walking on the grounds of an old run-down mansion, in the depths of winter under a foreboding grey sky. The gardens lay dormant and lifeless with an array of decayed plants bedded in the soil. Even though I was frightened, I kept walking. Then I suddenly realised that my body was no longer solid. It had become a shimmering mass of white crystalline light. And, although I was still in the shape of a physical person, this light radiated far beyond my body, touching everything that I passed. As I strolled by the flowerbeds, shrubs and trees, they all came alive with the most beautiful spring colours when they were touched by the light. The house also became fully restored. In particular, I remember an enormous tree in the centre of the lawn, covered in a profusion of delicate white blossoms tinged with pale pink. Everything about this tree was captivating. I was mesmerised by the sheer size of the tree and the surreal otherworldly splendour of the petals. It was as if the iridescent light of the Universal energy flowing through me brought new life to everything in its path. This reinforced the message that the beautiful crystalline light that I tapped into during my NDE is the Source from which everything is created.

In the final vision I was shown a large 3-D

representation of my brain. As the full-spectrum, holographic image rotated slowly before me, I could see the healing taking place both internally and on the surrounding tissue. I saw clearly how all the energy I had connected with during the NDE was restoring my brain to health. More than just healing, my brain was being fundamentally restructured. Previously inactive parts were now awakening to the Universal Consciousness to which I had connected. I knew that I had to have faith, to trust in the Divine healing process and to surrender to this wisdom.

These visionary experiences helped me to cope with everything that was happening and to focus my energy on making a full recovery. They reinforced the understanding that I received during my NDE that love is the only truth at our deepest core level.

The greatest gift from the whole experience is being able to feel this blissful love while in a physical body here on earth. I felt a continuous connection with this energy and still do to this day. By choosing to *feel* love, I naturally feel the love of Universal Consciousness flowing through me. Through shifting my thoughts from my head to my heart, I can go into this loving state instantaneously, anytime and anywhere. Sometimes I feel this love very powerfully, at other times it is more of a gentle flow. I believe that it is possible for everyone to feel this unconditional love, because this is the Source from which we all originate. I discuss this in more detail in parts 2 and 3 of this book.

◉ ◉ ◉

When my friends visited me in the hospital, I tried to share the essence of this NDE: the blissful love and joyousness of the whole experience. Many of them said that they could sense the beautiful serenity around me. It was not necessary for me to try to explain the inexplicable, or how I felt physically restricted but spiritually unbounded. Even though it was challenging to speak because it was so difficult to form sentences, no words were required because they said that they could feel this energy for themselves.

About ten days after the brain haemorrhage, as I walked slowly along a hospital corridor, I noticed a poster on the wall with the words, 'Be still and know that I am God.' During my experience with healing from the CFS I began to learn this. However, after my NDE I finally realised this truth: we are all part of the Universal Consciousness, Divine Wisdom, God's grace, infinite energy or Heavenly vibration, whatever terminology you wish to use. We all come from the same source of energy. Our greatest challenge is to become still enough to experience this truth. One of the ironies of this experience is that by lying in bed with restricted physical movement, I achieved total spiritual freedom! We run around in life, looking for happiness and fulfilment outside of ourselves, most often in places where it can never be found. In truth, it is within us, all of the time. I believe that each and every one of us can access the most extraordinary frequency of love.

From my NDE, I gained a deeper insight and understanding that life is everlasting. It flows to eternity.

We continue to exist after our vital life-force leaves our body. My experience was that my soul continued, but simply in another form. This was the 'Eternal Life', the 'Life without End' that I had learned about as a child in school. Looking back on this now, 'The Kingdom of Heaven is within you', 'Be in this world but not of it' – all these quotations from Scripture finally made sense. Even though I had rejected these teachings earlier in my life, I now understood their value in portraying powerful messages about a Higher Consciousness.

The NDE also reminded me of a line from the poem, 'Sailing to Byzantium' by the poet W.B. Yeats:[16]

> *An aged man is but a paltry thing,*
> *A tattered coat upon a stick, unless*
> *Soul clap its hands and sing, and louder sing*
> *For every tatter in its mortal dress.*

At the moment of death, although we shed the coat that is our physical bodies, our souls still continue to exist. This is our core truth, our essence, whatever language you wish to use.

◉ ◉ ◉

My NDE was caused by the life-threatening medical condition of a subarachnoid brain haemorrhage. Although the NDE was a magnificent spiritual experience, physically it was extremely challenging for my body. It was as if 5,000 watts had charged through a 50-watt bulb. It was really quite astounding to see how quickly my whole body reacted to preserve and redirect the energy to where it was essential for making a recovery. I just needed to listen, attune to and not try to hasten the pace of nature.

For a few weeks following the brain haemorrhage, I had a continuous pain at the back of my head. The constant headache was accompanied by a spasm in my neck, pulling my head backwards. Although with the passing of time, these symptoms slowly eased, I still felt some pressure at the back of my head. This gradually waned over the following six months.

In addition, my cognitive skills were severely compromised. As a consequence, I could not read anything. Even a fashion magazine, filled with lots of photos, became a jumbled blur as the letters and words faded in and out, somersaulting all over the pages. It was also difficult to construct sentences and hold conversations because I could barely piece words together in a coherent manner. Furthermore, my memory for names became impaired. This was bizarre, because I could generally remember everything about a person but not their name. It was frightening, not knowing if or when my cognitive abilities would return. All of these abilities did eventually return, with the exception of my memory for names. I still struggle with this.

The feeling of nausea remained with me for another week. This was not only an unpleasant feeling, I was also anxious that the physical act of vomiting might trigger another haemorrhage. I found that by breathing slowly I was able to move more easily through these waves of nausea.

All my senses became heightened to the extreme, which is a very common symptom following a brain haemorrhage. As a consequence, I became unusually sensitive. It was as if I were a crab that had lost its shell, going through the transition period before growing a new one. There was absolutely no outer casing or shield from the world. Everything was permeable and passed straight through me.

Another symptom following the subarachnoid cerebral haemorrhage, and from having to lie in bed from dawn until dusk, was that I found it difficult to sleep. Often, I lay wide awake throughout the night. As it was too intense for my hearing to listen to any music, even relaxing or classical music, all I could do was just stare at the ceiling. I remember it was made from squares of off-white-coloured foam tiles with varying patterns of small black dots. I stared and stared at those squares throughout the days and the nights, looking at the shapes and configurations of the dots. Rather than dwelling on my physical incapacity, I chose instead to imagine myself as one of those tiny dots, and being part of the infinity of Universal Consciousness. This helped me to focus my attention on integrating with the energy I had experienced during my NDE. I recognised that we are all part of this vast expanse, with each and every one of us forming an integral part of the whole.

I felt strongly that once I had passed through the immediate danger of having another haemorrhage or a stroke, I would regain my health. Unlike the CFS, for which there was no treatment or clear prognosis, the brain haemorrhage was a condition from which I believed that I would make a complete recovery. I was told by doctors that it would be possible to do this in a relatively short period of time of six months to a year, as opposed to several years. Nonetheless, I knew that I would have to surrender and allow my body to heal.

At the early stage of recovery, only family members were allowed to visit. However, my friend Lisa had other ideas. She was determined to see me, so she pretended to be one of my sisters. Usually when people came into my room they were quiet and in a hushed, gentle tone asked me how I was feeling but Lisa was having none of that. In she stormed, with her hands on her hips. She stood at the end of my bed, looking me straight in the eye, as she said, 'What the hell are you playin' at, Róisín? We're all worried sick about you.' Lisa has the biggest heart of anyone I know and she pulls no punches. This was her endearing way of saying how much she cared about me. I thought this was hilarious and began to laugh until I became constricted by the pain in my head. Lisa was on her way to the airport, heading off for a six-month trip to Latin America. I wished her all the best for her journey. She wished me all the best for my inner journey. I promised her that I would be a 'rebooted and upgraded version' of my former self upon her return. I knew that I would make a complete recovery, and then some.

While I was in the hospital, my mother found it very difficult to cope with what was happening. The whole situation was extremely stressful for her. When she called one of my sisters to tell her that I was ill, she said only that I had 'a bit of a headache'. Initially, my sister thought there was nothing to worry about, until a few sentences later Mum mentioned bleeding. When my sister asked if I had had a brain haemorrhage, my mother responded, 'Yes, dear, yes.' My sister came to see me every evening after work and would simply hold my hand as I lay in the hospital bed. She understood that it was too difficult for me to have a conversation. Her visits gave me something to look forward to, helping to break the monotony of the long, endless hospital days. I will always be grateful to her for her kindness.

My family and friends were all praying and meditating for me. I could tangibly feel the grace from their love and the power of their intentions. I distinctly remember hearing a loud drumming sound, and feeling a powerful healing vibration throughout my body, in a rhythmic manner, again and again, during my stay in the hospital. At times this was so intense that I nearly felt overpowered by the energy. It was only many days later I learned that a friend of mine had sent distant healing from Spain, with a whole group of people. They had used drumming as a means of sending the healing energy to me, which is well established in many of the ancient healing practices, including Celtic traditions.

One day, I received a surprise visitor. The paramedic, Kevin, popped his head around the door. 'Róisín, you made it – I knew you would.' Bounding across the room, he then crouched down beside my bed to talk to me, because I was unable to raise my head. 'I'm rarely sent to this hospital, but by chance, my ambulance was sent here today. I checked with admin to find out what happened to you and they said that you pulled through.'

'Thank you, Kevin, thank you for everything that you did for me.' I choked up while saying these words because I was so grateful for his kindness, at a time when I needed help. 'It has been an amazing experience. Life will never be the same again – that's for sure.'

We chatted for a few minutes. As he left the room, he turned back and beamed at me, 'Róisín, you have been through the worst. You will make a full recovery, just take it easy.' I listened attentively to his wise words. As it transpired, he was absolutely right.

Approximately a week after the brain haemorrhage, I was able to get up and walk a few yards. A friend of mine came to visit me and offered to take me for a short stroll. Off we headed along the corridor, as I wheeled my drip by my side. Although I was weak, I still managed to walk for about ten yards. You would think I had just climbed Mount Everest for all the effort it took. My friend patiently walked each step slowly with me, as I put one foot in front of the other. At the time, I was wearing the hospital's thick white TED (Thrombo-embolic deterrent) stockings that prevent thrombosis. These not-so-chic stockings came up past my mid-thigh. Out of the blue I turned to my friend. 'Honestly, tell me what do you think of the new range of stockings that I am wearing from the Victoria's Secret springtime collection?' He roared laughing as we continued to amble along the corridor.

◉ ◉ ◉

My need for independence soon came to the fore and I dearly wished to return to my home to heal. Thank goodness for my family and friends. They were marvellous. They stayed with me and developed a roster for arranging meals and medication every four hours, day and night. My home provided a safe haven for healing, and I knew that was where I needed to be.

During this time, I received so many cards and letters from friends wishing me well. I was deeply moved by the letters and have kept them all. I was so grateful for this outpouring of love and support. It really buoyed me up and kept me going during the recovery phase. In some ways it was like attending my own funeral. Many said they were shocked that I had been in a life-threatening situation. In Western society we rarely discuss death. As a consequence, people avoid looking at their own mortality unless they are forced to do so. Some friends candidly told me that through my experience they found themselves staring death straight in the eye and it frightened them.

I felt fortunate to have survived the brain haemorrhage and to be alive. I also felt humbled that I could still experience the beautiful, blissful soul connection from my NDE. I knew my life would be completely different going forward. After having such a profound spiritual experience, I was aware that I would take an entirely new path. Although I had no clue what this would look like or how it would manifest itself, I knew that I had to surrender to the process and allow my body to heal. I could not rush or try to predict the outcome. This was not easy, but I learned that my job was to let go, 'surrender to the bliss', and allow this energy to guide my life.

Kevin, the paramedic, called in to see me when I returned home. He was checking on my recovery and making sure that I was taking it easy. I gave him an ivory orchid to thank him for everything he had done for me. He returned the gesture with a beautiful wooden candleholder that he had carved himself. Replete with knots and age-lines representing the life of the wood, I will always treasure this perfect symbol, reminding me to keep shining the light throughout my life.

Conor and George, my friends from the CFS days, were brilliant. The three of us cried laughing when I told them how I had landed myself in this latest mess, by literally asking for it! I can still see Conor smirking with a huge sarcastic grin on his face, clapping his hands as he gave me a mock round of applause. 'Well done, Ro, bravo! BRAVO! BRRRRRAVO! Be so careful what you ask for next time and remember to use the words gently, please!'

Especially dear to me were the words my mother had said on the day of the brain haemorrhage. She looked at the paramedic as he closed the door of the ambulance, when they transferred me from the first hospital to the neurosurgical hospital. I heard her say, 'Mind Róisín, she is precious to us.' I cherished this, as I had always felt I should never have been born. It is reassuring to know that we are truly loved by those who are nearest to us. We all yearn for that deep sense of belonging, to be accepted for who we are. After my NDE, I realised that I did have a *raison d'être*, and not only from my own family. I was blessed to receive this gift when I became aware that we are all part of the loving oneness of Universal Consciousness.

This unconditional love is the true essence of who we are. It is within all of us. This is the energy that comes through each and every one of us. This is what we share with one another. All we have to do is become still enough to feel this energy. It is not necessary to have an NDE to experience this sense of oneness, just a willingness to be open to the possibility of its existence, and then to be guided on our own unique soul's journey.

I began to truly understand the meaning of the greeting *Namaste*, the Sanskrit salutation, whereby the Divine essence of one soul is acknowledged by the Divine essence of another soul. In Irish, we have a similar way of greeting people, *Dia Dhuit* (pronounced *dia gwitch*), which means 'May God be with you,' and the response is *Dia is Muire dhuit* (pronounced *dia iss mera gwitch*), meaning 'May God and Mary be with you.' This is similar to Namaste, as the Divinity in one soul recognises the Divinity in another. Thus the love and light of my soul greets the love and light of your soul. It transcends the human behaviours and so-called differences and comes straight from the heart. Ultimately, we are the same, from the same Source of love and light, irrespective of the differences that play out in our lives at the human level.[17]

The degree to which we choose to connect with this love and light determines how we live in this world. We all consciously or unconsciously vibrate at a certain frequency. If we come from a place of inner peace and soul connection, we emit a positive frequency out into the world. If we are not as connected, we may be emitting a lower frequency and unconsciously projecting negative energy. I became extremely sensitive to this phenomenon and still am to this day. As a consequence, I am acutely aware of the energy that I am connected with and radiating. I am also aware of the energy of people and the world around me.

Every person who has an NDE experiences their own unique journey. It has been extensively researched and documented that people tend to have experiences which would be similar to their religious or spiritual belief or background. During my NDE I was brought beyond the beliefs of my Christian upbringing. The all-encompassing blissful waves of love that I merged and became one with exceeded anything that I could have ever imagined, conceptualised or believed with my mind. Above all else, I learned during my NDE that we are all created from pure love. We are all created from the one powerful Source energy which is brimming with bliss and joy.

By far the most prevalent experience of people who have NDEs is a positive one, they tend to be life-affirming. Many people share that they felt welcomed on their journey towards the light. They describe being surrounded by a tranquil serenity and the whole experience was more 'real' than anything ever lived prior to the NDE. Although this was also my experience, I have heard of other people having NDEs which, although transformative, were not so affirming. I understand that many people experience a unity with a Higher Consciousness, but in some cases people may also receive a wake-up call as to the priorities in life. I recently heard the story of a man who was shot in the heart while working on the wrong side of the law. After he experienced an NDE, he totally changed his life. As it transpired, he lost his 'job' as an enforcer with his criminal gang. He had become useless to them because he had actually become 'all heart'. Even his girlfriend ditched him because he had lost interest in everything of 'substance', in other words money and material possessions!

According to the Dalai Lama, 'we cannot hope to die peacefully if our lives have been full of violence, or if our minds have been mostly agitated by emotions like anger, attachment, or fear. So if we wish to die well, we must learn how to live well: hoping for a peaceful death, we must cultivate peace in our mind, and in our way of life.'[18]

My intention in writing about my NDE is to share my experience as an inextricable part of the eternal light. I hope to share how I learned that at a soul level we are all equal – there is complete equanimity of all souls. By focusing on living life, here and now, with an understanding of this eternal light, the purpose of this book is not in any way to romanticise death but simply to show what is possible when we face our fear of death. We become free to create our best lives.

Initially, having accessed this bliss and harmony, I thought that my life thereon would be peaceful and without any struggles. However, as a consequence of my NDE, my whole energy had shifted dramatically in a short period of time. I became much more aware of the energy of the world around me. Looking back, I suppose what happened next was to be expected.

About six weeks after the haemorrhage, I remember feeling very lonely. It was extremely challenging to watch any form of anger or violence, even on the television. I became so upset seeing people constantly recreating pain out of habit, not knowing that there was a better alternative available. Since I did not know anyone else who had experienced an NDE, I felt isolated. After accessing the Higher Realms, returning to this world seemed so harsh and hostile. I honestly found it difficult to be here.

I decided to ask a dear friend, who was also a neighbour, for help. We sat talking for hours on the granite steps in front of my home, as the early morning sun broke through the clouds and tall trees. My friend spoke of how my life, as everyone's life, is a gift and I had the choice to see it that way. She also reminded me that the only way any violence in this world could be changed is by each of us changing from within.

She talked about how the darkness of violence, to whatever degree, cannot be banished by more darkness. It is only through shining our souls' lights that we all can create a more loving state. Fear, darkness and even evil can appear and feel very real in our physical world. But if we have faith, thus opening ourselves to seeing that which is invisible to our eyes, we can observe life from the perspective of our Higher Consciousness. With this expanded vision, we are shown that fear is the absence of love, darkness is the absence of light, and evil is the disconnection from our souls' deepest truths. At our essence, we are all pure love. She challenged me to have the courage to fully embrace the light I experienced during my NDE and live with this light in all aspects of my life.

Since then, I have spoken with other people who have also had NDEs and evidently these feelings are normal. As the post-NDE euphoric state begins to wane, and you realise that your sense of awe at the beauty of life is not shared by others, there is a period of readjustment to being back here again in the physical realm. I am fortunate to have become friends with an American woman who also experienced an NDE. Whenever we find ourselves going through a challenging time, we always laugh as we tease each other, 'Please remind me why I chose to come back here again?' Although I joke about this, at a deeper level I know why I came back: initially it was for my parents and now it is to fully embrace the opportunities and challenges of life, and to encourage the best in everyone on life's journey. I intend to savour the exquisite joy of loving and living every moment.

As with my experience of CFS, I would not change one moment of the brain haemorrhage or NDE. This time though, I was able to appreciate it as a wonderful opportunity while I was living the experience. I received so many gifts that I will have for the rest of my life. Paramount among these gifts is access to the inner strength that comes from knowing that we are all one with the powerful infinity of Universal Consciousness. This is a humbling experience but also a great realisation that this energy can be consciously tapped into at any moment in time.

It took about one year for my body to grow stronger and fully integrate this new energy. Throughout that year, I consciously focused on rejuvenating through rest, meditation and healthy food for my body to be able to accommodate this Higher Source of energy. When I was strong enough I swam in the sea opposite my house. In the early morning, with the sun low in the sky, a beautiful channel of light appeared across the water, at the foot of the rocks. On the surface of the sea, this channel glistened as if thousands of tiny mackerel leapt into the air and splashed back down into the water. Below the surface, the light shone through the jade-green water onto the waves of sand on the seabed, sculpted by the motion of the sea.

As the light penetrated through the water, it danced in unison between the gentle rippling waves of the sea and the carved waves of sand on the ocean floor. The fusion of light and water created fine lines of vivid, multi-coloured hues, traversing each other, forming and reforming a kaleidoscope of patterns in continuous motion. When the sand was disturbed, it kicked up crystalline flecks which became suspended by the buoyancy of the water and slowly twisted and turned, reflecting light in every direction. Every time I swam into this shimmering channel, surrounded by the light, I relived the beauty of my NDE. This daily ritual reinforced my beautiful connection with the Heavenly eternal light here on earth.

I feel so grateful for this integration of the physical and spiritual realms. I am blessed to be still in a physical body that is fully healthy and yet have access to this amazing 'Heavenly' connection. I enjoy all the pleasures of the physical senses making life here beautiful – the taste of delicious food, seeing the beauty of nature, hearing exquisite music or birdsong, being touched by a friend's love, feeling the warmth of a fire – all while experiencing this profound peace and serenity.

Being aware that I can always be in touch with this energy by changing my thoughts so that they come from love, I consciously choose to feel love in my heart as much as possible. When I do this, I naturally reconnect with Universal Consciousness and my life flows beautifully in a serendipitous way. When I forget, life feels strange, off-balance and I know that I need to become still to reconnect with this empowering Source of love.

Ironically, having faced death has given me complete freedom to live life. When I look at what is the worst that can happen, well, I have already been there and it was brilliant! When my time comes to leave my body in this physical realm, I will embrace 'death' with the full knowledge that life truly is everlasting. I will enjoy returning to the unbounded expanse of my soul, free from any physical constraints. Please understand that I don't have a death wish to throw myself into a bull-ring with a rampaging horned animal any time in the near future. I simply wish to fully live before I 'die', by living every precious moment with an open mind and open heart. I want to integrate as much of this energy into every aspect of my life by constantly expanding to accommodate more of my soul in this human form.

Each one of us can strengthen our souls' connection every moment of the day, if we choose to open our hearts and tap into this infinite Source of pure love. With a childlike sense of wonder at the beauty of life in its various forms, life can be such a magical ride when we can feel and experience it by living from our hearts.

A few months later, my brain haemorrhage was categorised as idiopathic in origin – in other words, the source of the blood leakage was never found. Even though it was not possible to explain medically why this occurred, I knew deep in my soul why it happened. I am grateful for the gift of the brain haemorrhage because from my near death experience, I received the gift of life.*

---

* Approximately 10-15% of subarachnoid brain haemorrhages are not caused by an aneurysm. From the recent but limited research available on this subcategory of sub-arachnoid haemorrhages, it appears that these types of brain haemorrhages have a far better prognosis. So the doctor was right, I was one lucky lady!

CHAPTER 4

GIFT OF SHARING
THE LIGHT

As a result of the NDE, my perception, not only of our physical world but also my understanding of the non-physical world, is forever changed. I now view everything in terms of light and energy, both in this realm and the afterlife. As a consequence, I have changed my life to become a visual artist because, through this medium, I hope to share the beauty of the eternal light in a way that people can feel it in their own lives. I came across a wonderful quote from the playwright, George Bernard Shaw: 'You use a glass mirror to see your face. You use works of art to see your soul.' This is my intention with creating art – for people to see the reflection of their own souls' light. I also learned recently – after I had already been working with crystal for many years to emulate my experience of the light during my NDE – about the frequent use of crystal and glass in ancient Irish legends as metaphors for describing the surreal nature of the 'Otherworld'. It was as if all the crystal pieces sewed seamlessly together linking the past, present and future – a reflection of the ethereal 'Otherworld', mirrored in this physical world. I will discuss this in greater detail in chapter 7.

After my experience during the NDE, when I gained an understanding and awareness that all forms of matter at the basic level are made from energy, I truly understood the life-force behind our thoughts. I realised that we are created from energy and, in this physical form, we all vibrate at a certain frequency. Indeed, our thoughts mould this energy, which is why it is so important to focus on the positive, and to approach every situation with gratitude and love.

With this in mind, I wanted to have some inspiring art to create a joyful and uplifting ambience in my house. I decided to try and recreate this for myself.

Using remnants of white silk left over from when I made my curtains, and some loose clear glass crystals, I hand-sewed the crystals to the silk, to keep their lucidity, as any form of glue would compromise their ability to shine. I thoroughly enjoyed creating the artwork and felt centred and connected throughout the whole process. When it was finished, I stretched this onto a large canvas and hung it on the wall in my sitting room.

As I looked at the piece, I saw a stunning reflection and refraction of light as it danced across the walls of my sitting room. The artwork appeared to have a vibrancy and life of its own. It created enchanting swirls of multi-coloured light, and I realised that I was remembering the beauty of my NDE. I became enveloped once again in the blissful energy. By having had the faith to trust in Divine Grace, approximately one year after the NDE, my life's purpose became clear.

I knew from that moment on how I would tap into my soul to share the sacred light from my NDE. I was overjoyed to be able to share the beauty of this experience, in a direct soul-to-soul language, through art. I called one of my dearest friends and asked her to visit my home. I did not say anything to her but simply showed her my artwork. Her eyes lit up when she saw the piece, and with a huge smile on her face, she exclaimed, 'This is how you will share the light! You will be guided and supported on this journey. Trust, Róisín, trust.'

People often ask me if my art is religious. I always answer that it is not *per se*. Each artwork is inspired by the connection with the unconditional love of Universal Consciousness that I experienced during my NDE. This theme of love is the basis of all the major faiths. When we look at the cornerstones of world religions, the various forms of Christianity, Judaism, Buddhism, Hinduism, Daoism, Islam and Shinto, to name but a few, we see that they are based on love. Having grown up in a country where for decades and even centuries, in the Northern province, people killed each other, invoking religion for the cause, I believe strongly in the love which transcends divisions and focuses on that which brings people together.

When I was at the start-up phase of creating this art, I contacted one of my former professors at Trinity College Dublin, Prof. William Kingston. Fifteen years after graduating, I was touched that he remembered who I was, and he could not have been kinder to me. I was unsure if I should go ahead with creating this art, as rationally it made no sense at all. However, when he saw my work, he smiled and said, 'There is much more to this art than meets the eye, isn't there?' Then he continued, 'So many people have unique and innovative ideas but lack the courage to go through with them. If you can find the resources both within yourself and financially, Róisín, follow your dreams. You will never regret at least trying and I truly believe that this will work.' Over the next few months he provided guidance on practical issues relating to the art, and whenever we met he would never accept any form of payment for his advice, not even a gift of chocolates or wine. He would simply say, 'make a success of this art, share it with as many people as possible, this would be the greatest payment of all.'

After designing more artworks I began exhibiting my art at numerous venues in Dublin, including the Royal Dublin Society (RDS) and a gallery in south County Dublin. I then took the leap of faith and decided to take a large solo stand at Ireland's premier art show at the RDS. The art was well received. Soon thereafter, I realised it was time to bring my art to the United States. This was a giant step. However, I believed that the energy of the artworks would resonate in America and I would be able to share it with a much wider audience. I understood that the United States would form an integral part of the journey for sharing the light through the medium of my art.

My first exhibition was at the New York Art Expo 09. In my total ignorance of the art world, I had no idea how difficult it would be to exhibit in New York, let alone import 20 artworks from Ireland. Looking back, this was a blessing, as I had no mental blocks to making it happen, and serendipities started to occur.

One day at the Expo, a grey-bearded man in his seventies, wearing a pair of worn jeans and check shirt, came over to see my artworks. He smiled as he studied my art in great detail. His name was Harry Nasse. I later learned that Harry owned the second-oldest gallery in the art district of Soho, in Manhattan. Harry, who is a kind and gentle soul, has devoted his life to helping artists show their work, and I was delighted when he offered me a solo exhibition at his gallery a couple of months after the Expo. I returned to Ireland in the intervening period to prepare for the upcoming exhibition.

I will always remember when I flew from Ireland back to New York for this exhibition in Harry's art gallery. I sat in the departure lounge, feeling scared as I waited to board the flight. Having an exhibition as an unrecognised artist in the city of New York was a daunting task and a huge financial risk. It was also a lonely time, as I hardly knew anyone in New York. However, by having faith in Divine guidance, I trusted that I would be shown the way.

Just then, on the wall in the departure area, I saw a photograph of Loretta Brennan Glucksman, Chairman Emeritus of the American Ireland Fund. Loretta has worked for many years to raise funds for projects to assist peace in Northern Ireland and to help numerous charities throughout the island. I thought how lovely it would be if I ever had the opportunity to meet her. Little did I know that I would be given this opportunity within less than a week.

When I had arrived in New York, I had requested an appointment to meet with Niall Burgess, the Consul General of Ireland in New York. He kindly met with me and offered to help in any way he could because he is a great supporter of the arts. He introduced me to the editors of all of the Irish-American newspapers, magazines and radio. Thanks to his introduction, Loretta Brennan Glucksman learned about my art and wished to interview me on Irish Radio New York.

When I arrived at the recording studio I felt nervous, as I had never been interviewed before, least of all on radio. Loretta was so professional and relaxed that within a few minutes I felt completely at ease. From her extensive involvement with the arts, I knew that she would understand my work and interest in sharing the light. While we conducted the interview at a beautiful mahogany table in the recording studio, the conversation flowed. We could just as easily have been sitting around a kitchen table drinking tea, as we chatted about my art and the source of inspiration. Loretta encouraged listeners to come to see the exhibition and attend the opening reception.

On the opening night of my exhibition, Niall Burgess, the Irish Consul General, gave a wonderful speech. He accurately described in detail the pre-Celtic archaeology which was the inspiration for some of the artworks, because he had studied this at university. He also recited a poem by Seamus Heaney to accompany the theme of the exhibition. I felt humbled that he had taken so much time, in his busy schedule, to provide me with such generous support.

I also received great encouragement at my second major exhibition in New York from Roma Downey and her husband Mark Burnett. Although they live on the West Coast of the United States, they happened by chance to be in New York the weekend of my opening reception.

An almighty clap of thunder accompanied by a flash of lightning announced their arrival as they managed to rush into the gallery just moments before the heavens opened in a torrential downpour. We all laughed together at this providential entrance!

Roma, best known for her role in the series *Touched by an Angel*, is a remarkably inspiring woman. Despite her challenging upbringing during 'the Troubles' in Derry, losing her mother when she was only ten years old, and her father a decade later, she has blazed a trail of light throughout her life as an actress and producer. While in her presence, I fully understood why she has been so successful – she has a profound faith which guides her through life.

Mark is equally inspiring and also shares Roma's powerful faith. A former member of the British Army, and now a successful television producer, he seems to have an ability to galvanise those around him. When they are together, it is a true blessing to feel the warmth of their presence. We spoke openly that evening about light and our purpose in life. And I was touched by their generosity of spirit when they encouraged me by buying an artwork for their home, but way more importantly, when they were leaving, Mark turned to me and said, 'We are backing you, Róisín.' Those words were spoken with such sincerity that I knew this was another sign that I was on the right track. Up to this point, I had been flying on a wing and a prayer, with blind faith, as I had listened to my inner guidance. I had felt very isolated, as if I were on a narrow path of a steep mountain cliff and I could only see a few steps ahead of me. However, deep in my heart, I knew it was the right way to go. I trusted that if I kept going, a clear path would appear.

I have been blessed that not one but many paths have appeared for sharing my art. There has been tremendous kindness shown to me by many people, in particular the Irish-American community throughout the United States. Previously, I had no idea of the dynamism and spirit of co-operation which exists in this community. I think it originates from the shared experience of coming to America, where these emigrants or their ancestors came off the boat (or nowadays the plane) and found themselves in a foreign land, surrounded by strangers, with limited financial resources, knowing that they had to make it work.

As a consequence, everyone helps each other in real and practical ways.

The spiritual community in America has also been very welcoming. I met Deepak Chopra on numerous occasions and he has always shown a true generosity of spirit. Dr Chopra has opened the minds of so many people in the Western world to the healing potential and the wisdom of Eastern philosophies.

I have also been blessed to meet one of the greatest visionaries and most influential women of our times, Marianne Williamson. The first time we met, I gave her a piece of art as my way of thanking her for the invaluable guidance I received through her books, which had been the catalyst for change in my early adult life. I simply cannot imagine what my life would be like now if I had not been fortunate enough to read *A Return to Love* at that pivotal stage of my life. When she saw my artwork, she quietly whispered, radiating a beautiful smile, 'This is soul art.' Since then we have met several times, including when she came to my exhibition in Washington, D.C. and for lunch in my home near Dublin. Marianne has strongly encouraged me to continue sharing the light through my art. I am beyond grateful for her continued support and loving presence in my life.

Within a couple of years, by the autumn of 2011, my art was well established in New York. I was fortunate to have had five exhibitions in Manhattan in less than two years.

When the opportunity arose to have another exhibition at the Consulate General of Ireland on Park Avenue, Bill Whelan, the composer of *Riverdance*, came to the opening reception. This was a full-circle moment from when I was ill with CFS in my twenties and was inspired by the passion of *Riverdance*. If you had told me all those years earlier when I was bed-bound in a darkened room that I would meet the composer of *Riverdance* at the opening reception of my art exhibition in New York, I would have laughed at the mere suggestion. This really proved to me that Divine Wisdom has a much greater vision for our lives than we could ever comprehend with the restricted thinking of our minds.

Nonetheless, life can unfold in wondrous ways when we let go and surrender. I thanked Bill so much for attending the reception and also for his uplifting music, which had had such a profound effect on my life. With a lovely warm smile on his face, he said, 'Lots of people helped me when I was starting out as a musician, Róisín. I am more than happy to be here for you.' His kindness meant the world to me that evening.

From the first exhibitions in Ireland, to the New York Art Expo and the exhibitions at the galleries in Manhattan and at the Consulate, I was privileged to share the light of the art with people of all ages and cultures and from all walks of life.

From 2009 to 2011, Manhattan became a second home for me. All of this was made possible because of the generosity of Dr Christine Ranck. Christine and I met on my first visit to New York when I was exhibiting at the

Art Expo 09. She has co-authored *Ignite the Genius Within*, the best-selling book on creativity, and consequently has a keen interest in all forms of art. Christine described to me how, when she first turned the corner at the Expo and saw the illuminated artworks, she was intrigued, and especially so when she watched other people stop in their tracks mesmerised by the display. She asked me lots of questions about my art. At the time, we spoke about how the light I accessed during my near death experience inspired my work.

On my next visit to New York, Christine and I met up many times and we became the best of friends. She invited me to stay in her apartment on the Upper West Side. Since then her apartment has become my unofficial home in New York. I am grateful to her because this gave me a foothold in Manhattan and a home away from home. Christine and I have become dear friends. She often accompanies me to the Irish-American receptions in Manhattan. So much so that I tease her that we will have to find some Irish blood in her. In the meantime, her adopted name is Christine O'Ranck!

I am equally grateful to my friends in Washington, D.C. many of whom I knew from my days in Geneva. They also made me feel completely at home. While on exhibition during 2011 and 2012, I was supposed to stay with one friend for a week, but after a few days we laughed so much together that he asked me to remain on at his house for the full two months. He jokingly refers to my sojourn as the 'Celtic week', as he congratulates me on truly having merged with the sense of 'timelessness' from my NDE!

The first exhibition in Washington D.C. was opened by
the Irish Ambassador to the United States, H.E. Michael
Collins. He spoke eloquently about the exhibition,
Irish arts and culture. I was grateful for his kindness,
as he offered his assistance with exhibiting my art in
the United States. Since then it has been a joy to be so
warmly welcomed throughout the United States, as
more doors opened for me in Dallas, Chicago, Boston,
Albany, Connecticut and also on the West Coast. I am
always a combination of excited and nervous as I head
off to a new city, knowing hardly anyone yet with a kind
invitation in hand.

As I have gone in my life from student status, to
diplomatic status, to well below student status again by
becoming an artist, I appreciate the simple luxury of a
warm welcome and a home-cooked meal. As a dear friend
once said to me, 'You are on a budget of a leprechaun's
shoestring!' I truly was. Yes, that was the extent of my
budget, but I had a greater fortune that no amount of
money could buy – a wealth of amazing friends. Thanks
to kind invitations, I managed to keep self-financing
the exhibitions in America. I am so grateful for their
heartfelt generosity. I gifted artwork in lieu of rent and
was welcomed everywhere on my travels.

Many people said that I would never make it as an
artist. They said that it could not be done. It was almost
impossible to make it work. Rationally, they were right.
If you look at statistics of the rate of success for people
starting their own ventures, approximately two out of
three fail. Then, if you look at artists who can actually

make a living from their art, oh my Lord, it is abys
However, I knew this was not about me, but about a
Universal energy that flows through me. As long as my
intention was clear on sharing the light I experienced
during the NDE, then this energy would flow beautifully
and I knew deep in my heart and soul that it would work.

Even though it made no rational sense to create this
art and bring it to America and beyond, there is a lovely
quotation by the French artist Henri Matisse: 'In art,
truth and reality begin when you no longer understand
anything you do or know …' It was time for me to trust
my instinct and follow my heart.

Although it was challenging to self-finance the
exhibitions, I decided to use my savings and to live
a simple life, in order for my money to be used for
developing my art. Even though Dad would have
much preferred me to get a 'sensible job', to show his
support he gave me his silver writing pencil to sketch
my designs. This writing instrument must be 60 years
old if it is a day, and has marks where it is worn from
use, because my father wrote with it his entire working
life. I felt as if he were passing the baton on when he
gave this gift to me, wishing me all the best with my new
venture. I treasure this pencil and still use it to this day
for sketching my designs.

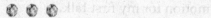

It is generally recognised that the two biggest fears in life
are death and public speaking. I had overcome the first, so

it was time to conquer the second, and if this would help with sharing my art, then I would do my best. Initially, it was challenging for me to speak in public because when I was growing up in Ireland, as children we were taught not to 'blow your own trumpet'. It was and still is part of our culture not to self-aggrandise. In many ways it is a good trait. However, I knew that I had to overcome this inner fear to share my deepest truth about the light.

Although I had given numerous presentations while working at the European Bank, they were about issues relating to privatisation in Eastern Europe. This was, relatively speaking, easy because they were fact-based and non-emotional. Even when they were in French – *pas de problème*. As a very private person, sharing the depths of my soul with an unknown audience is a completely different matter. However challenging it would be for me personally, I knew that as soon as I opened up to the possibilities, opportunities would become available. And, sure enough, they began to appear.

My friend Alex in New York suggested that I contact two of the main holistic centres in Manhattan to see about speaking engagements. Within a couple of days, when we were walking in downtown Manhattan, we bumped into the manager of one of these holistic centres. As Alex knew her, he introduced me and the wheels were set in motion for my first talk.

The following day, when we were again walking in Manhattan, we happened to meet the director of the second holistic centre. Once again, because Alex knew this person, he was able to introduce us, and the door was opened for me to speak at this venue. Alex was flabbergasted, as this was clearly another example of providence at work. He turned to me and said, 'We're on a roll, girl. If we are this good at manifesting, let's start thinking about George Clooney right now!'

The first talk took place that very weekend at the holistic centre's annual health seminar. The day before the seminar, the director contacted me to say that the speaker for the 3 p.m. slot had cancelled at the last minute and would I take his place? Oh my goodness, be careful what you ask for. Here we go again.

With two large pieces of art on display behind me, I spoke without using notes, to maintain eye contact with the audience. As this was my first public speaking engagement, Alex sat in the front row, like a secret conductor. He used hand gestures to indicate when I needed to raise or lower the volume of my voice, or adjust my pace. Like most people, I felt nervous before I went on stage. However, as soon as I allowed myself to simply be a conduit for sharing the light, it all flowed beautifully. This was thanks to Divine Grace, and the help of Alex's conducting skills! Extraordinary assistance is available to us all, if we choose to simply go still and listen to the wisdom of Universal Consciousness and allow this to guide our thoughts, words and actions. From this experience, I truly understood how I could overcome ordinary fears with this extraordinary help by allowing myself to trust and connect with this light.

When I spoke at the second holistic centre, a couple of weeks later, there were only five people in the audience. Whether there are five or 50 people, I always give my heart and soul, as the people who come to the talk have so generously given their time to hear about the inspiration for my art. On that occasion, one person in the audience was Dr Carol Smyth. We connected immediately because Carol, who is also a graduate of Trinity College Dublin, has a keen interest in NDEs and the afterlife.

After the presentation, a member of the audience remarked that she had been on my website and felt that the images of my artworks were not capturing the dynamic effect of the light on the crystals. She suggested that I should have a video of my artworks on my website. Carol offered to ask a friend of hers to see if she might do this for us. A few days later, Carol kindly arranged for the production of a professional video of my art with her friend, Christiane Arbesu, who was vice president at a division of PR Newswire at that time. Little did I know what was to come next. This video was distributed as part of a PR Newswire press release that was simultaneously picked up by over 30 newspapers and journals throughout the United States. Overnight, my art had been shared throughout America. In addition, an image had been posted on a large electronic billboard on Times Square!

Carol and Christiane had arranged both the video and press release as gifts for me. They told me that they really believed in what I was doing and wanted to assist me in any way they could. I will always be so grateful to them. A few days previously, when I had set the intention to share my art in New York and the United States, in my wildest dreams I never could have imagined this outcome. This experience taught me that through being clear in my intention, and aligning with Universal Consciousness for everyone's highest good, amazing and wondrous things really can happen.

By connecting with and surrendering to the Higher Consciousness that is available to us all, the Divine plan can unfold naturally and manifest in this material 'reality'. This plan is always much bigger and has a greater vision than any we can ever have with the narrow thinking of the rational mind. In this case, I had not set a specific goal but created an all-encompassing intention, and then handed it over to Divine Wisdom to arrange the details of how, what, where and when for this to happen in the best interest of all concerned. When this was the result, I truly understood that expectations of specific outcomes or defined results can be very restrictive, as they are limited by our mental perceptions. Intentions, on the other hand, are infinite as they open our lives to boundless possibilities.

As a result of that talk with five people in the audience, my art was now being shared throughout America. The same invisible hand that held me so safely when I needed to recover from the brain haemorrhage was now opening doors throughout America for light to be shared through this art.

● ● ●

Within a few short months, I was invited to be a guest speaker in New York at the United Nations Staff Recreation Council Enlightenment Society. It was an honour to speak there, and the experience evoked memories of my days of working at the UN in Geneva. This was again one of those moments in life when my professional past merged with my present, to create the future of sharing my art.

A year later, I was given the opportunity to speak at the Conscious Capitalism Conference (CCC), near Boston. The CCC is an annual event for senior executives who wish to run their companies in a manner that creates a positive contribution to society. Michael Gelb is the creative director of this institute, and even though the schedule for the conference was already packed, Michael was determined that I should speak on the main stage. 'It would be wonderful to share your story with this audience, Róisín.'

'Yes, Michael, it would be great but how are we going to manage this?'

Michael has the largest smile of anyone I know, it practically touches his ears. As he grinned, he gave me that knowing look, 'Guess who is the MC today?' taking both hands and pointing to himself. 'I'm the boss on this stage. You're on!'

Michael is a professional public speaker and he also knew that I was a novice – so he took a gamble on me, one for which I will always be grateful. Michael sat in the front row, beaming up at me throughout the whole talk. I was delighted to have the opportunity to speak because the ethos of CCC is perfectly aligned with the intentions of my art. Many people approached me after my presentation and it was a joy to learn more about the different ways people are working to raise the consciousness within their companies and organisations. Steve, the videographer, kindly edited my speech and sent it to me by email as a surprise. 'Here's a gift for your website, Róisín, good luck.'

In the autumn of 2011, when my art was on exhibition at the Consulate General of Ireland in New York, in addition to being a guest speaker for numerous Irish business organisations, I was asked to share the artworks with 60 male students in their early teens from All Hallows High School, in the Bronx. The students came from challenged economic and social backgrounds and the education they were receiving at All Hallows was important for shaping their future. I remember thinking: what can I say that these young men would be interested in hearing? How could I connect with them? Most importantly, I knew it was not about what I would say but how I would listen. I wished to hear all about their fears, joys and especially their dreams, hopes and visions for their lives.

The chairman emeritus spoke to me about the school's mission to give these young students the best of education, so they could further their prospects in life. He had asked me to describe my NDE and talk about the gifts of life and education, to really encourage them to be grateful for the opportunity they were being given at the school.

I took as my theme 'The Power of Choice', and how, irrespective of external circumstances, we always have the ability to choose how we respond; literally 'respons-ability'. I gave the example of my decision when I was in the ICU. At a time when I appeared to be at my most helpless and vulnerable, this was in fact when I made the greatest decision of my life. By choosing not to go into fear but by deciding instead to focus all my attention on being in the moment, I accessed a powerful light within. I wished for the students to be able to relate this to their own circumstances and instead of feeling powerless by situations, to feel more empowered in their lives.

After preparing my speech, I had all the key points in my head. I intended to talk for about 10 to 15 minutes. However, these students seemed fascinated by the energy of the artworks. They were inquisitive to learn and understand more. Their questions continued until we ran out of time. I became increasingly aware that these boys were on the cusp of manhood, and at a turning point in their lives. One student told me about his hopes for his professional life. He was not sure if he wanted to be a psychologist or an artist. I asked, 'Why not be both?' He beamed back, 'Yes, I will!' Another student asked about the sacrifices I had made in order to be an artist. I told him that materially, yes, I had made sacrifices, but in terms of the joy I feel in my life, I am blessed beyond belief.

At the end of the talk, another student came up to me and tugged on my sleeve. 'Ms Rose, Ms Rose,' he whispered in my ear because he did not wish the other students to hear. 'So no matter what is going on in my life, I can always choose how I respond ... Tears of sadness and tears of joy, they are not the same but it is alright to shed them both, isn't it?' I barely managed to keep myself together and not well up in tears myself, as I encouraged him to be in his truth no matter what was going on in his life. 'Yes, sometimes we need to go through the sad tears but if we stay in our own inner truths, I promise tears of joy will eventually follow.'

At this time, I was nearly at the end of the two-month exhibition at the Consulate. Although always grateful to be able to share my art, I was feeling exhausted. The work included a full schedule of curating by day, arranging all the publicity, organising receptions, attending evening events and also juggling all my emails and telephone calls. I was questioning if I could keep going.

Just then I unexpectedly received a large envelope in the mail. It contained hand-written letters from the students. Their words filled my heart with joy. These young men inspired me to move forward with my art, as they explained in their letters how the energy of the artworks had touched their lives. My intention had been to give them hope for their future and a sense of their own potential to move forward with confidence. However, they were the ones who gave this very gift to me!

Whenever I give talks, I always have to be careful when I explain the source of inspiration for my art. The mere mention of the word 'death' brings up many people's deepest fears. I see faces freeze in front of my eyes. It can be the fear of their own mortality, fear of the afterlife or fear that there is no afterlife. It might bring up grief from the loss of a beloved family member or dear friend. Often I rephrase it as a 'near-life experience', as initially this is not quite so challenging. When I explain that the NDE was truly wonderful, and it has given me a second chance to live life from the heart with no fear of death, then people tend to be able to relate to this and want to learn more.

Usually as the talk progresses, I can see fears dissolving and hearts opening. Most people want to live a joyful and happy life. By connecting with the light, we naturally know how to love and be loved. We also recognise that we have a purpose and meaning for our brief time here on earth. Frequently, by the end of the talk, people are so receptive and open to the experience that many often come up to me and say, 'I would love to have a brain haemorrhage and NDE too.' But I always give a gentle reminder to be careful what you ask for, you just might get it!

I love sharing my art with people as much as I love creating art. My life alternates between two very different kinds of existence. Overall, my life is in balance – just made up of two extremes. When I share the artworks, I run around foreign cities, hosting exhibitions, giving talks and attending receptions. My days often extend into the early hours of the morning. These are times when I have some of the best in-depth conversations with interesting people. I particularly love meeting new people from different cultures and learning about their stories, because everyone has a unique perspective on life. And, when I create artworks at my home by the sea, this is a contemplative, silent and quiet phase for me.

Through the creation process, I go into a near-meditative state, as I become grounded and energised again. This replenishes my soul for then sharing the art, and the cycle continues.

Over the years through sharing my art, I have been blessed to meet inspiring men and women of all ages and at all stages of the ups and downs of life. Many people have commented, without knowing the story behind my art, that these images are what they would like to see when they die, while others feel an inner peace, lightness or even a sense of jubilation while viewing the art. Just as every person's soul journey is unique, every person's experience of the art is individual.

I especially love sharing artworks with children, because they are naturally open to connecting with their souls' wisdom. Their freedom to express truth is so refreshing. My cousin relayed an amusing story to me of his experience one day when he observed two small boys running around and stopping to look at my artwork in the lobby of the National Concert Hall in Dublin.

'I love the sparkling light. They're real diamonds, aren't they?' the younger boy said to his older brother.

'No, don't be silly, they're crystal.'

'Ah, that's a pity, are you sure? I thought this was a posh place!'

If someone had told me a few years ago that I would be an artist, with numerous exhibitions across the United States, I would have never believed it to be true. This has all happened not because of me but through me. I am 'in-spirit', inspired to create my art. Then, with 'entheos', enthusiasm (meaning with God), I share my art. Without expectations or attachment to outcome, I am still astounded by the opportunities that appear.

Once I have set the intention to share the beauty of this love and light, I leave it up to Divine Wisdom to sort out the details of how this manifests. I do not attach to the outcome, but trust and am open to the people and the opportunities that appear. Some doors open easily, others take a while longer and some do not open at all. Whenever this happens, I place my trust in Divine Wisdom and know that the best outcome will always be created. What often occurs is that later an even better option materialises, which I was not able to see at the time. I have learned to surrender to this Higher Consciousness and be guided, remaining receptive to the unfolding opportunities.

When I set my intentions at the beginning of this venture I had two priorities. The first was to share my art in public venues, where people could relax and feel inspired to connect within to their own souls' truths. The second was to donate art to raise funds for different charities. I have since found it to be so true that when we give unconditionally we receive in unimaginable ways. As our hearts open through giving, we receive more grace and blessings in the most unexpected of ways.

I truly believe that it is the responsibility of each one of us to find this light that is shining within, no matter how faint a glimmer it may appear to be at times. By allowing ourselves to remember the times in our lives when we loved what we were doing and to feel this emotion over again, we set the intention to reconnect with this inner light. If we choose to come from our hearts and share this love with everyone we meet, then we live our true calling by allowing this love to flow through us, in our own unique way.

The infinite bliss of unconditional love and eternal light is the core essence of who we really are. And, each and every one of us has a purpose and a reason for being here. Whether we are lawyers, stay-at-home parents, accountants, farmers, physicians, or artists, it is not necessarily what we 'do', but who we willingly want to 'be' that matters most. This also applies to all areas outside of our professional lives, by how we contribute to society through volunteering or helping those more in need.

Through tuning into our hearts and the wisdom of Divine guidance, we naturally find our true calling. Whenever we are filled with an exhilarating feeling of joy, then we know we are singing to our own souls' tune. Similarly, when we lose all sense of time, especially when we are giving to others by contributing in a positive way, we know that we are on the right path.

CHAPTER 5

GIFT OF LOVE

From my NDE, I became acutely aware that we are all pure energy. Each and every one of us is a spiritual being, temporarily residing in a physical suit of skin and bones. Knowing that our true essence is love and light has greatly simplified my life.

During my NDE, the answer to every question that I asked was always the same – love, a resounding, definitive response as waves of pure, unconditional, blissful love permeated my very core. So now, rather than focusing on the multiple dilemmas of all the quirks and foibles of the human condition, I choose to simply come from the heart by asking: *what is the most loving choice now?*

In the years following my NDE, I have embraced this energy and usually feel centred and connected. When my whole body feels alive, vibrant and joyous, then it is in alignment with love and my soul. If I feel heavy, weighed down or depressed at the thought of pursuing a particular direction in my life, then I know it is not my soul's truth. By becoming still and connecting with my inner voice and the message from my soul, I know whether I am in the right place or if I need to take an alternative path. We all have this inner compass available to us, every moment, if we choose to follow our souls' guidance.

Luckily, my parents taught by example what a healthy relationship can be. They were the best teachers of love, life, loyalty and laughter. Dad used to always say that the key to a great marriage was to just say, 'Yes, Dear.' He was half in jest and whole in earnest. However, this was not in a self-sacrificing way, but a genuine sharing from the heart. They both loved each other and wanted the best for each other. This was what I was expecting marriage to be. Not to agree all the time but to have open and honest communication, while being willing to find a way to work together, with each person sharing from their heart.

During the summer of 2007, I began dating a friend of mine whom I had known for over 20 years, since our first year in college. There was great joy and happiness in our relationship, which had been built up over years of friendship. We were very much in love, thoroughly enjoying each other's company, with lots of shared interests

in life. After a few months, we decided to get married. I
thought we were going to have a wonderful married life
and, at a deeper level, become spiritual partners together.
Our wedding took place in November 2007.

I completely trusted my husband, as we had been
friends for so long and honesty had never been an issue.
However, within a couple of months of marriage, it
became apparent that something was very wrong. The
situation worsened over time. With each passing week
and month, the person I had known as a dear friend and
had trusted, was slowly disappearing.

The situation escalated until two years into our
marriage, when I learned a painful truth about my
husband's finances, which had been concealed from me
since the beginning of our marriage. Although initially
I became numb as part of me did not want to hear what
was happening, I had to quickly come to terms and deal
with this. Over the following months, I hoped, prayed
and wished for the person I had known for over 20 years
to return, but as each day passed it became clearer that
this was never going to happen.

The harder I tried to keep our marriage together, the
clearer it became that I would never be able to trust my
husband again. The main issue was not the huge financial
loss which now affected both of us. Far worse than this
was the betrayal of trust which by this stage had become
irreparable. We had chosen the beautiful lines from the
poet W.B. Yeats as part of our wedding ceremony, *'I have
spread my dreams under your feet; Tread softly because you tread
on my dreams'*. With the passing of time, those indelible

dreams became crushed, along with any remaining hope for what could have been a great married life together. As I gradually allowed myself to feel the full depth of this pain, I was devastated and utterly heartbroken.

The sacred marriage vows we wrote together to 'love', 'trust', 'cherish', and 'respect' were broken, yet I was still bound by law to stay in this marriage because it takes five years to obtain a divorce in Ireland. Feeling trapped by this situation, I chose to ask for Divine guidance and to be open to the answer. There is a wonderful line by Albert Einstein, 'You can't solve a problem on the same level that it was created. You have to rise above it to the next level.' So rather than focusing on the problem where my mind tried to grapple with the conundrum as to why this was happening, I chose to be open to the solution. The answers came, when one amazing synchronicity appeared after another, providing a clear pathway to exit this marriage.

When I was looking for Divine guidance for my marriage, it happened in the most unexpected of ways – in the dying moments of my mother's life, which I discuss in more detail in the next chapter. I experienced what is known as a 'shared death experience'.[19] I once again felt the bliss I had experienced during my NDE. The love that infused the entire room, in her last few moments of life, was so palpable that I could almost touch it. There was a lightness, an incredible, nearly trance-like feeling of lightness, with a profound peace.

I have since heard of many people also experiencing 'shared death experiences' with the passing of a loved one. At those moments in time, on the cusp of death, the energy becomes so intense that any uncertainties about the real priorities in life disappear. Like a laser beam, life becomes clearly focused. I knew that it would be impossible for me to be true to myself and stay in this marriage. I was unable to place trust in my husband and instead of having a solid foundation in our relationship, I felt like I was sinking in quicksand. I had the choice to stay in a marriage because of legal constraints, added to the societal and religious convention, or to listen to the truth of my soul.

During the few days following my mother's death, I was given more Divine guidance, when one evening, as I walked by my bookshelf at home, one of my favourite books caught my eye. After removing it from the shelf, it fell open on the page about making decisions and handing them over to a Higher Consciousness for guidance. When I went to bed that night, I asked to be shown in my dreams the best direction for me to take in this relationship.

That night, I dreamt that I was in a wooden boat, floating on the calm surface of a lake. The lake was surrounded by trees and as I looked around, everything had a strange grey/green hue. Even the sky was dark and overcast. Then, without any warning, the boat unexpectedly overturned. I suddenly found myself thrown into the icy water. Thrashing my limbs, I desperately tried to stay afloat. But my attempts were futile, as I found myself being dragged down into the depths of the lake. The deeper I descended, the darker and darker it became, until I was engulfed by pitch-black water. Unable to catch my breath, I felt like I was suffocating. I realised that if I did not detach myself from the boat I would drown. I unleashed myself and slowly buoyed up to the surface.

When I woke up from this dream, I was shivering with a coldness in the core of my being. I felt that I had been given a clear message to leave this marriage, but I wanted to remain open to further guidance.

Later that day, I went to look for the book *The Distant Shore* which was written by author Colm Keane about Irish people's near death experiences. Colm had interviewed me for his book, so I knew that the story of my NDE was going to be included. In the bookshop, I was astonished when I saw the cover of the book. It was the exact same grey/green lake scene as the image in my dream. There was one person in a wooden boat, rowing away in the distance. I knew this was a clear sign to cut myself free and steer my own life.

Although it was heartbreaking, I knew that I could no longer stay in my marriage. Once I made this decision, I remained open to seeking the solution and I was so grateful when it appeared in my life. Through a series of synchronistic events, I learned that I would be able to end my marriage in a British court within a few months, instead of a difficult and lengthy five-year process in Ireland. This was a truly amazing outcome and one which was unforeseen. Nine months later, my divorce was finalised and I was given the freedom to start a new life for myself.

It is well known that we can become either 'better' or 'bitter' from every challenging situation in our lives. The last thing I wanted was to be bitter in any way so I made the choice to keep my heart open, no matter how painful it was. Ultimately, I realised that the choice lay within my own mind and, most importantly, within my own heart. By choosing to see the whole situation through the loving eyes of my soul, I kept my intention on attaining inner peace and joy by making the decision to come from love, no matter what the external situation looked like. I chose to love myself enough to remove myself from this situation which was no longer tenable, to let my husband go with love, always wishing the best for him in his future life, and to stay connected with the deepest truth of the unconditional Divine love throughout this whole experience.

So many fears and raw emotions, from anger to grief, came up as I journeyed on this path. I decided to experience all of them, so I could let them go. Eventually the overriding feeling became one of sadness for the loss of what could have been a great marriage. It took quite some time for this sense of loss to pass.

I was also fearful about being able to trust again, not just in relationships but friendships too, because we had been friends for such a long time before we were married. As I began to question all my friendships, I quickly realised that the person I needed to trust the most was myself, and also Divine guidance.

I focused on feeling the pure love of Universal Consciousness that I had merged with during the NDE, this energy that had healed my body during the brain haemorrhage. Although this time the challenge was a relationship, as opposed to my physical health, I had learned from the experience that at our deepest essence, we are all light-filled energy beings. If we retain any negative thoughts or emotions, these are like patchy shadows, tarnishing and obscuring the light we radiate out into the world. So I knew that by releasing any negative emotions about this situation, I would clear myself, setting myself free to create my future.

Even though I knew that the most empowering gift I could give to myself and my ex-husband was the gift of forgiveness, it was still challenging. I continuously made the decision, over and over again, to release the emotions and only see the truth of the Divine Light within myself and my ex-husband. Eventually, with the passing of time, a profound peace and gentle compassion gradually emerged from the depths of my soul. By keeping the faith, I was given this beautiful gift which allowed me to move on with my life.

It was intriguing to see how this healing physically manifested in my body. During the following months, as I let go and released emotionally, I gradually lost the extra weight that I had accumulated while I was married. Without any change in diet or exercise, it simply fell away. Unconsciously, I had added this as a protective layer, and when I no longer needed it, I shed the outer casing and re-emerged as my true self. Those nine months prior to the granting of my divorce were like a rebirthing in so many wonderful ways.

During my marriage, particularly for the last few months, I had felt like an elastic band pulled backwards, extended and stretched to my absolute limit. I felt pulled and pulled until I had nothing left to give and I almost reached the breaking point.

Yet, when my marriage was over, one of the surprises was that, because throughout my marriage I had always kept the intention of coming from the love of my soul, the momentum of the accumulated energy caught up with me in the most wondrous of ways. I suddenly found myself catapulted forwards in all areas of my life, both personal and professional. My life took off in ways that I could never have envisioned possible. It was as if all the accumulated soul's energy had waited in the wings, and as soon as I became free again it poured through me, creating joy in my life once more.

I also chose to reaffirm everything for which I felt grateful – paramount of which was my newfound freedom. By focusing with gratitude on the positives, I was able to move through the pain and heal more quickly. By making self-healing my priority, over a year after the end of my marriage I was fortunate to date a wonderful man when he unexpectedly appeared in my life. Gentle, caring and loving, he was truly Heaven-sent. Although initially it was challenging to experience the vulnerability of opening my heart again, I chose to move through this. Otherwise, I would have been entrapped in the past to the degree to which I was unable to unlock my heart. With tender compassion and affection, we nurtured and encouraged the best in each other by creating a supportive environment filled with joy, laughter and mutual respect. Together we entered an inner sanctum where the external world was suspended and our core essence revealed itself. He provided a safe space for me to become my true self again and I will always be grateful to him.

Another year later, I knew that I had reached the place of being at peace. When I can laugh at a situation which had previously been extremely challenging, I know that I have let it go. On this occasion, I was out for lunch with a good friend of mine. She was happy to see me fully embracing life once again. She smiled as she said, 'Well, Róisín, you were the Tin Man, Scarecrow, Lion and Dorothy all in one. You had a big heart to get married, a big brain to leave the marriage and huge courage to keep going to find your way home.' As luck would have it, I just happened to be wearing my red shoes that day. I stood up, and with a big grin I clicked my heels and said, 'There's no place like home!' We threw our heads back and laughed.

The truism that everything I had been looking for could be found within resonated with me. Instead of searching for joy from outside, by becoming still, this love naturally emanates from the infinite wellspring of love within. It was so freeing to fully realise that my happiness truly comes from reconnecting with the depths of my soul and Universal Consciousness.

If we understand that we are energy beings responsible for the energy we contribute to relationships, then the question is: *in what direction is our energy moving and flowing?*

CHAPTER 6

GIFT OF LETTING GO WITH LOVE: DEATHS OF MY PARENTS

We all know that life is about change, yet we crave the stability of the status quo. One of the greatest challenges we face is that of letting go with love, when a loved one dies.

My parents had given me everything throughout my life. There was little that I could ever do to thank them in return. So I was grateful for the precious gift from my NDE of having no fear of death, and to be able to share this with them as they departed this life.

One of the Gaelic ways of saying 'May you rest in peace' is *solas síoraí* (pronounced *sol-as sheer-ee*) which when translated literally means 'eternal light'. It appears that this ancient culture understood that life does not end at the moment of death. Indeed, physical death may have been viewed as the beginning of a new journey into the light. During my NDE I learned that we are always part of this eternal light, both during our brief lifetime here on earth and also in the afterlife. It was a true blessing to be able to share my experience of the light with my parents at this time.[20]

During a ten-week period towards the end of 2010, both of my parents died. After my mother passed away from a long-term illness, my father died from a heart attack shortly thereafter. At the same time, I also ended my marriage. It was extremely difficult to cope with losing the three people closest to my heart within such a short timeframe. Instead of dwelling on all the negativity, I made the decision to focus on the moment and be fully present for my parents, so that I could assist them with their journey into the light, by helping to make it as comfortable and natural as possible.

I was honoured to bear witness to the rebirth of their souls. We cherish the occasion of the birth of a child, when the eternal soul becomes manifest for a short period of time in human form. However, the occasion of death is just as sacred, because this is when we return to our souls' full magnificence. The illusion of this world vanishes as we reintegrate with Universal Consciousness. Having experienced during my NDE that there is no such 'death' in the way that is generally perceived by modern Western society, I am at peace with their passing over. I know that life is everlasting and believe that they have merged with this eternal light – *solas síoraí.*

❂ ❂ ❂

In the latter years of my mother's life she developed dementia. For anyone who has witnessed this disease in a loved one, it is truly heartrending. We were fortunate that most of the time, even when Mum was confused or did not know who we were, she knew that we were friendly, so she was never frightened of any member of the family.

On a few occasions, Mum became fully lucid and I clearly remember one in particular, three months before she passed away. On that day I was given a gift beyond measure by her full presence for about 30 minutes. It was as if the fog had lifted and through that sacred opening Mum returned, filled with her humour, wit, wisdom and invincible spirit. Mum was back. I could barely contain my excitement. I was so grateful for the opportunity to thank her.

I thanked her for everything that I could think of that she had done for me throughout her life. As memories flooded into my mind, I listed them for her in a stream of consciousness. I knew this would probably be the last time I would speak to Mum and she could go away again at any minute.

From the heart I began, 'Thank you, Mum, for your kindness when I was scared on my first day at school, for bandaging my cut knees every time I fell, for collecting me from school in the pouring rain, for always telling me to 'stand up to a bully', for not allowing myself to be walked over, for teaching me how to cook spaghetti Bolognese ...' Disjointed and unrelated, it did not matter, even the actual memories themselves were not necessarily that important, all I really wanted Mum to

know was how grateful I was to her. I continued, '...
for spending hours helping me with my homework, for
encouraging me to go to college, for showing me how to
crochet and sew ...'

At this point my mother interjected, with a faint smile
as she reminisced. With her clear blue eyes focused on
mine, ensuring that I heard her soft voice, she began to
speak, 'Róisín, be sure to continue with your art and
don't mind the rest of them who tell you not to do this.
Live a happy life. You have so much joy ahead of you.'

Then to my amazement, she proceeded to speak of
issues that were concerning me, and there was no rational
explanation as to how she could have known about these
worries. It was truly remarkable. She told me that she
was proud of me, as she was of all her daughters. Then
I could sense that Mum's spirit was leaving, so I quickly
interjected. 'I love you, Mum, I love you ...' And with
those last few words she was gone again.

We shared a precious half hour together that day,
as mother and daughter, and then it was as if the mist
rolled back. That was our last clear conversation.
Although physically present, looking back I wonder,
was my mother's spirit already departing? Was she
going in and out of the other realm, and that is why she
was so serene?

On 21 September 2010, I was called and told that my
mother had received the last rites from the priest when
he visited her in the nursing home. We had five beloved
days with Mum before she died. Even though she was
very ill, she had a calm and tranquil presence. I wished

for her to let go and leave behind the limitations of a body which could no longer support her beautiful spirit. I truly wished for her to be free.

Over these days, Mum would sometimes whisper a few words about her mother and father or dear friends of hers who had passed away. There was a faint smile on her face, as if she were greeting loved ones. As she looked straight ahead, was she seeing people that she recognised? Maybe they were connecting with her, ready to welcome her, as she was about to make her transition to the light?

The nurses at the nursing home were all fond of Mum. They kindly created a warm, safe environment, making her as comfortable as possible. My sisters and I were able to visit any time we wished and stay as long as we wanted. This made a huge difference, as those last few hours closed in on us. As I walked into the nursing home the evening my mother died, the time 3.20 a.m. came into my mind and I knew that was when Mum was going to pass away.

There was a lovely nurse on duty and she let me stay with Mum. I spent those last few hours talking to Mum with my head on her pillow as she breathed up and down, just like I used to put my head on her tummy when I was a little girl and felt her breathing in and out. It was a special and sacred time. I told her how much I loved her and what a wonderful mother she had been.

I spoke to her about the beauty and freedom of being unrestrained by a physical body. I shared with her that she would experience a bliss and serene tranquillity beyond anything she could ever imagine. I promised her that we would take care of Dad and encouraged her to let go. My mother was spirited by nature, but this was a time for her to allow herself to let go.

At around 1 a.m. the nurse told me that Mum was dying. I contacted my family, who came to be with her for the last couple of hours of her life. Then at 3.20 a.m., on the morning of 27 September 2010, encircled by the love of her family my mother passed away peacefully.

In her dying moments I was enveloped by a similar energy to that which I had experienced during my NDE – *the oneness of pure love*. I now know that such experiences are called 'shared death experiences', though I was completely unaware of these phenomena at the time. Sensing the all-encompassing serenity and peace, it was a joy to feel this because I believe that Mum was embraced by pure love as she departed this life.

Mum was a Catholic who took great solace from her faith. We had often spoken about how, half an hour before she would die, the angels would come to collect her. They would surround her bed and then gently guide her away with them. I could certainly feel a loving presence, and I wonder was this my mother's experience of death?

Another reason I believe that Mum had a peaceful passing was that she had grown up in an environment steeped in our ancient Irish heritage, in the west of Ireland. She spoke fluent Gaelic and had read numerous books written in a style imbued with the mysticism of our legends. She had a deep spiritual connection and felt this in her heart. As a consequence, when it came to dying, I wonder was she able to embrace passing over with more ease and peace due to her understanding of the 'Otherworlds'?

Mum's cousin celebrated the funeral Mass accompanied by the angelic voice of hymns performed by a family friend. As the soothing tones resounded throughout the church, sunlight shone through the stained glass window. I remember watching light penetrating the cobalt-blue-and-yellow-tinged glass, creating an aura of peace in perfect harmony with the music.

Friends and extended family all attended the Mass. There was a tremendous outpouring of love for Mum. It was a clear, crisp autumn day and the sun shone brightly as we drove around the Hill of Howth with Mum's coffin. She used to love the scenic drive, so we took this route to the graveyard, for one last time. Then we lowered her remains into the ground and wished for her to rest in peace.

For a few weeks after my mother passed away, I could sense her presence around me. It was as if I were wrapped in a cushioned bubble, shielding me from the outside world. I felt nurtured by a soft, warm energy which enveloped me. This gentle comforting feeling which surrounded me softened the blow of her death and gave me the strength to face the following weeks. I felt completely safe and protected. In her younger years my mother was a strong woman. After she died,

I continued to feel her strength as a powerful guiding presence. This feeling remained with me for a few weeks, fading in and out, passing through phases of increasing and decreasing intensity.

Within a week of Mum's funeral, we knew that Dad had to go to the hospital, as he had developed serious symptoms. I can still see the expression on his face when I told him that we needed to go to accident and emergency. He looked at me in disbelief. My father did not like hospitals at the best of times, but making this announcement in the middle of the Ryder Cup, to my dear dad, was unthinkable. I became *persona non grata* instantly.

What made it worse was that two of the main players on the European team were Irish. Rory McIlroy and Graeme McDowell were both playing for Europe and this was a huge honour to have two Irish golfers on the team. McIlroy was already playing his match on the golf course, and McDowell was just about to tee off at the first hole. Reluctantly, Dad agreed to come with me, but on two conditions. First, that I record the golf competition for him. Second, that I would take him home as soon as possible and care for him. We shook on this and the deal was done.

Over the next few weeks, life for my sisters and I centred around Dad's hospital visits. I will always remember one day in particular when I went to see him. Mum's passing was so heart-breaking for him that I felt that he might have been losing the will to live. This was very challenging to see, as I loved my dear Dad deeply. He did not know that I could see him, as I quietly stood out of his line of vision, and I surrendered to the highest good for Dad and let him go with love. It was different releasing Mum because she had been ill for many years and at the end I wished for her spirit to be free. It was so much harder letting Dad go. Although he was 86 years of age, I had always assumed that Dad would live into his nineties like many of his siblings, but now I realised that this would be unlikely to happen.

The morning of 19 October, I was feeling very raw emotionally and low in my spirits because I had just ended my marriage. On the same day, I went into the hospital to see Dad and the nurse informed me that the oncology doctor had paid a visit. I looked at her and said, 'Oncology?' She said, 'Oh, you don't know, dear,' and took me aside into a quiet room. Surrounded by boxes of bandages and medical supplies, I leaned against the plinth for support as she spoke softly, relaying to me that Dad was going to die within a few short months at best. Dad did not know himself and I did not want him to receive this news on his own. I stayed in the ward for as long as possible, waiting for the doctor. When I was with Dad, it was so difficult to keep the tears back, yet I did not want him to see me crying. I said that I had a cold, excused myself and cried my eyes out in the bathroom. When I regained my composure, I came back to Dad and focused on keeping myself together while I was speaking with him.

That same day, at the Royal Dublin Society in Dublin, there was a lecture on the topic of how to live in the present moment. I decided to attend the talk. When I arrived, I found a quiet place to sit upstairs on the balcony, away from the crowds. As I sat there I barely heard a word the speaker said but I felt the energy in the room. I focused all my attention on being fully present in the moment and connecting with Divine Wisdom. This was how I had coped with the brain haemorrhage, moment by moment, and I chose to do the same again. It was a gift to be reminded of this, at such a crucial time.

When it was clear that Dad was going to die, all I wished for him was that it would be an easy death, as I did not want him to suffer in any way. I hoped that he would not be in pain and enjoy a good quality of life in his last few weeks. I wanted him to pass over easily and be reunited with my mother, if that were his soul's wish.

I wanted to be sure that he knew how much I loved him and how thankful I was to him for being such a great father. Although Dad and I would have hugged a lot, in all the years we had never said 'I love you' to each other. I also knew that if I did say it directly to him, it would be a mutual acknowledgement of his pending death. So, as a way of saying it to him but without directly saying 'I love you', one day I looked at him and said, 'I love you to bits, Dad. You're the best.' He smiled at me with loving compassion in his eyes and responded, 'I love you too.' Then he took a deep breath and continued, 'Now that's sorted', with a big grin on his face.

I am so grateful I had the opportunity to say this to him.

We run around in life, with all these high-tech ways of communicating, through texting, mobile phones, emails etc., yet ironically the *quality* of the communication, the ability to sit, face to face, with those nearest to us and tell them how much we love them can so easily get lost in the chaos. In a couple of sentences, we had each said from our hearts how much we loved each other, and no more words were needed.

It is so important to know that we always have the opportunity to communicate our love to those who are dear to us. We can do this person to person, if they are still here in the physical realm. Or, if they have already passed over, we can send loving intentions with our thoughts, and thank them for all they gave us while they were physically alive.

After a couple of weeks, Dad was increasingly restless and just wanted to be at home. However, it was essential for him to be in the hospital for care. At this time, he was moved into a ward with two beds. As I pushed his wheelchair into the room, the gentleman in the other bed greeted him with, 'Welcome to the penthouse suite!' This was perfect, as Dad was obviously going to be sharing the room with a comrade-in-arms. I warned his fellow patient that he would need ear plugs because of Dad's loud snoring, to which Dad retorted with an impish grin, 'I don't snore and I am sure of that because I have never heard myself snore!' The other gentleman laughed. The two of them were great company for each other for the following ten days. So much so that as soon as this man was discharged from the hospital, Dad insisted upon leaving too.

Even though the doctors wanted to keep my father in the hospital for another few days, his mind was already set on going home. When his attending physician came to see him, Dad shook his hand but did not let it go. He kept saying, 'Thank you so much for all your kindness, now it is time for me to go, and my daughters will take care of me.' The doctor said that he did not wish to keep him there a minute longer than necessary. Dad looked at his watch, then looked at the doctor and with a big smile said, 'The minute is up!'

He did this in such a humorous way that the doctor gave in and discharged him. Once he was discharged, my father was in the wheelchair and down the elevator faster than a Formula One racing driver. When we sat in the car before I drove off, I looked at Dad and asked, 'How did you manage that?'

He replied, 'I don't know, but drive fast and let's get out of here.' I am a fast driver and Dad used to constantly tell me to slow down. However, on this occasion, he would have willingly let me break every speeding limit on the way home.

With each passing day, it was apparent that Dad was getting weaker and weaker. The local doctor, hospice and community nurse were all terrific. My cousin and aunt, who are both doctors, also supported us by answering lots of questions so we could make Dad as comfortable as possible. My sisters and I wanted Dad to have everything he wished for and to feel loved and cherished. We all helped in minding Dad, cooking meals that he would enjoy, even if he could only eat a tiny portion. Dad was a gentleman to the end, always appreciative of everything that was done for him.

The day in the hospital when we both said that we loved one another, we had also accepted that he was facing death. I totally respected that Dad would approach me in his own time and in his own way about the subject of death – when he was ready.

A week before he passed away we were talking in his bedroom. Sitting in a chair below the main window, he was wearing his cosy fleece dressing gown with a blue check blanket wrapped around his legs. Even though it was early in December, there was a clear blue sky outside and the sun shone through the window, bathing us in warm rays of light. After we chatted for a while, the tone in Dad's voice changed and I knew that he was ready to broach the subject of death. In a hushed, almost inaudible whisper, he asked, 'Róisín, have you connected with Mary at all?'

'Yes, Dad, I have. Sometimes I can sense Mum's presence strongly when I feel a soothing or comforting sensation enveloping me. I believe that she is peaceful and in a great place now.'

He let out a huge sigh, 'Oh, that is wonderful news to hear, wonderful, absolutely wonderful.'

Dad was delighted for Mum, as he truly wished to know that she was alive, in some form. We then continued to share a beautiful conversation together based on my father's Catholic beliefs, as was the tradition of his generation, and on my experience during the NDE. Merging his religious beliefs with my loving and compassionate experience during my NDE, we spoke about the afterlife. As the conversation flowed, I could see him becoming lighter in himself as he opened up more and more to the reality of an afterlife. I sat with Dad and listened as he shared his hopes about the eternal life. As we continued to talk, his breathing became easier and lighter, his physical demeanour changed as he sat more upright and confidently in his chair. By the end of the conversation, he was more peaceful than I had ever seen him before. He looked directly at me as he said, 'There really is hope, a hope everlasting ...'

In the early hours of the morning, at around 1.30 a.m., on the 10 December, I heard Dad stirring so I went in to see if he needed anything. He asked me, 'Róisín, could you turn the light off for me, please?'

I was puzzled by this because the light was not switched on in his room. The only light that I could see was the amber glow from roadside lights outside the bedroom window. 'The light is not on, Dad, are the street lights bothering you? I can pull the curtains if you wish.' It certainly did not register with me, because I was half asleep at the time, that he was talking about *the light one experiences at the cusp of death*. I kissed him goodnight on the forehead and went back to bed. An hour later, I heard some noise from his room again. When I went in to check on him I realised that he was having a heart attack.

'Let go, Dad, let go. Mum will be there for you, she is waiting for you.' I called for my sister and we were both with him for the last few moments of his life.

Over the next few hours, I had another 'shared death experience' after my father passed away. I lay down on my bed, connecting with Dad's soul, visualising him going through to the light, seeing Mum and his relatives again. I kept this as my focus. 'Go to the light, Dad, it is safe for you to go.' Then, at around 10.30 a.m., I experienced a huge sense of peace and tranquillity. Maybe this was when he had connected with the light?

Even though Dad was no longer with us in physical form, I believe that his spirit was still close to his body. I distinctly remember seeing shimmering, vibrant colours surrounding his body when he was laid out in the open coffin. Many relatives came to our home when Dad's body was laid out, before we brought the coffin to the church. The 'wake' is important because it recognises that, even though the person is physically dead, the soul still lives on in the eternal light – *solas síoraí*. It is a way to honour the soul by taking the time to pay respect to the deceased person and also accompany their soul so they are not alone on their journey to the afterlife.

Even though it is a poignant time, it can also be an occasion to celebrate the person's life.[21] During those few days, I spent as much time as possible sitting beside

Dad's coffin, both at home and by going to all the Masses in the church on the Sunday. I wished to be there to support him in every way possible.

Similar to Mum's funeral, once again the church was filled with family and friends, all there to remember my father and pay their last respects. Mum's cousin celebrated a beautiful Mass and spoke of how my parents were reunited once again in Heaven.

It was so touching on the day of his funeral to see staff who had worked with Dad for over 30 years tearfully saying, 'There will never be the like of him again.' I knew that I was totally biased because I was Dad's daughter, but I realised at his funeral that many other people felt the same way about him. He was dearly loved by his family, friends and work colleagues alike. There was no greater testimony to a life well lived.

My friends were wonderful. I remember some of them standing speechless, not knowing what to say as they gave me a big hug. Just being there was all that mattered. It meant so much to know that my friends cared at such a difficult time, by their willingness to show up and provide comfort, in whatever way they could. Some friends who had known Mum and Dad spoke highly of them both. Conor and George, from my CFS days, bastions of strength as always, came and said, 'We stick together during the tough times, Ro, we're always here for each other.'

It was a bleak, bitterly cold winter's day as we took the same scenic drive around Howth Hill to the cemetery to lay Dad's coffin in the graveyard beside Mum's. I stood rigid, frozen by the icy wind and numbed in my overwhelming grief, as I watched Dad's coffin being lowered into the ground. It was like a *déjà vu* of ten weeks earlier, when Mum's remains were laid to rest in the same grave.

Surrounded by my sisters, extended family and friends, I unexpectedly felt two arms encircling me from behind and clasping together in a tight grip around my waist. It was one of my dearest friends, Jules. She whispered into my ear as she squeezed me, 'You are not on your own, Ro, we are all here for you.'

Jules had been at the same cemetery a couple of months earlier. She was one of a handful of people who also knew that I had just filed for divorce. 'Hold on Ro, you're strong, you can get through this. Your parents will be with you for the rest of your life, as two loving angels on your right and left shoulders. They will guide you.'

I learned a few days later that my petition for divorce was accepted under British jurisdiction on the same day that I buried my father. This meant that my divorce would be finalised within a few months, as opposed to the lengthy five-year legal challenge in Ireland. Was Jules right, was Dad already guiding me from above, helping me to close one of the most painful chapters in my life, by granting me the freedom to start anew?

I get up, I walk, I fall down. Meanwhile, I keep dancing.
Rabbi Daniel Hillel

The next few weeks were surreal, as I tried to come to terms with the loss. I decided to go to the annual Christmas salsa party, in my usual red velvet dress. It was a strange, dreamlike experience as I spun around the dance floor, feeling so loved and supported by my friends but not knowing if I should laugh or cry. Not that I had any control over my emotions at this stage anyway. Losing Mum was heart-wrenching. Dad's death within weeks of Mum's was completely overwhelming.

Even though I have experienced an NDE and believe in my deepest heart and soul that there is an afterlife, nonetheless I still grieved the physical loss of both my parents after they passed away. Letting go of them to 'death' was so painful that I truly wondered if I could ever feel whole again. I burrowed deep within and found the strength to keep going. After they left, it was a particularly lonely period of my life. Although I can still connect with them spiritually, I miss their physical presence, just like anyone else who has lost dear loved ones.

All of this was happening in the context of being totally broken-hearted, as I had also ended my marriage at the same time. I had kept my tears inside, as I did not want Dad to see me crying in his final days. I had stayed strong and positive for him. But when it was all over, all those tears which had been shored up were released and they flowed like Niagara Falls. It was so cathartic to simply let go.

When I cried, the tears engulfed every part of my being. My heart was so shattered that I did not know when they were tears of sorrow from the loss of Mum or Dad, or from the loss of my marriage. All that I could do was literally go with the flow, surrender to the grief and have faith that I would get through this and come to inner peace again.

Another big freeze was forecast by the weather bureau, and I knew that I would be housebound for at least ten days. I made a deliberate decision to stay in my parents' home, in order to fully experience my grief. Before I could go to those depths, I first had to thank everyone who had been so kind to Mum and Dad, as I knew that my parents would have wished for me to do this on their behalf. After buying gifts of boxes of chocolates, I drove around the local area delivering them to the nursing home, family doctor's office, the community health nurse, hospital and also to a special woman, Connie, who had helped both Mum and Dad for years.

When I had thanked everyone, I then began the process of trying to pick up the pieces of my life and start healing. I knew it would never be the same again. I once heard that the more you love someone, the bigger the void they leave in your heart when they are gone. This was certainly the case. However, I chose to keep their memory alive without a hole in my heart but with the whole of my heart.

Every day I walked in the castle grounds and went to the dolmen where I had played as a child. I found a way of going across all the fields to come out at the other side of Howth, where the graveyard is located. I walked for about three hours every day in the snow, over to the grave. This made it much easier to allow myself to go through my grief.

The week just before Christmas, a notice came through the letterbox about a carol service in the local church. It was snowing that evening as I walked the short distance to the church. When I went in, the whole space was illuminated by candlelight and warmly welcoming. The choir was singing, 'O Come All Ye Faithful', in a harmonic chorus. This was perfect, reminding me of the true meaning of life.

A friend of mine, whom I had not seen in years, smiled and waved me over to sit beside him. He asked how I had been keeping. I briefly whispered to him about my recent losses. He kindly kept a watchful eye on me, while we sang our way through the service with a mixture of joy and sadness in equal measure. When it was over, we went for dinner at the restaurant in the grounds of Howth Castle. After the meal, we walked on the grounds of the castle estate. It was a clear night and the stars illuminated the sky. The fresh snow glistened in the fields under the glow from the light of the moon. It was so beautiful, being surrounded by a silent stillness. It felt as if the whole world had stopped and revered this quiet homage from nature.

In early January, I was in Dublin city centre when I bumped into my old boyfriend from my days at Trinity College. It was one of those beautiful days when there was not a cloud in the sky and the sun was so low, it shone directly into my eyes. With no notice, as I was blinded by the sun, he suddenly materialised in front of me. I told him everything that had happened and he was very supportive, saying it could only get better. At the time, I was barely able to walk, as all the stress had created pressure in my lower back. In addition, I had not slept well for months. Even though I must have looked like a train wreck, I always remember him saying that I looked great. He was either in dire need of spectacles or simply being kind to me; either way, it was much appreciated at the time. 'Everything will get better from here on, Róisín, hang in there.'

Shortly after that, my lower back became immobilised with pain and I was barely able to move. I believe that this was a result of all the grief. Mum and Dad had just passed away and my marriage to a man I had loved had ended. I felt that my back pain symbolised how the pillars of my life had collapsed and I had to rebuild myself with a whole new foundation.

I went to see a good friend of mine, who is a natural health practitioner specialising in back problems. I knew that she would help to realign my back so I would be able to become mobile again. As I lay on her plinth and recounted the previous few months, her sensitivity and compassion lifted my spirits and encouraged me to keep going. 'You will get through this and go on to lead a great life, Róisín, keep the faith.' She was absolutely right; keeping the faith was the key to moving forward.

Over the next couple of months, my family, friends and neighbours were a huge support, especially at times when the grief was quite overwhelming. I knew this was my soul speaking to me, telling me to be gentle with myself and rest.

All my friends, on both sides of the Atlantic, wove a safety net of love around me. They were all so wonderfully empathetic. They offered help in every way from providing hot home-cooked meals to a listening ear, as they lovingly nourished me, body and soul. I truly felt surrounded by so much caring tenderness from both the visible and invisible realms. A dear friend and counsellor, Betty Cosgrave, was a living angel. She guided me through all my emotions with such compassion. 'Listen to your whispering soul, Róisín, for all your answers come from within.'[22] One of my aunts was particularly kind, as she gently encouraged me to keep going. She reminded me, 'Life is so short, dear, make sure you live a full and happy one.' In her late-nineties, she truly leads by example. And Heather, my friend from years previously when I worked at the European Bank, also offered great encouragement. 'Grief, darling, is the price you pay for love. Dealing with grief never actually gets better, you just get better at it!'

At this time, I felt blessed to have a coping mechanism which was ingrained from my early childhood – a deep understanding of knowing how to navigate the ebb and flow of the emotions. In Irish the way we say I am sad or I am happy is, *Tá brón orm* (pronounced *thaw broan urm*) or *Tá áthas orm* (pronounced *thaw awehass urm*), which literally means there is sadness on me, or there is happiness on me. I grew up with this understanding that my feelings can be separate from who I am. This was invaluable when I was going through such a sad time in my life. When a wave of grief hit me, I was able to let go, feel all the emotions, and ride the wave, flowing with the emotions, knowing that I would eventually be able to arrive safely back at shore. I understood that my feelings did not have to drag me down like an undercurrent below the surface where I would struggle with life. The emotions did not define me, yet they were a part of the whole. By letting them wash over me and through me without resistance, I was able to feel them in every cell of my being, and release them in order to be able to move on, heal and start living again. I chose to remain open to feeling and experiencing the pure love of my soul and Universal Consciousness with which I had merged during my NDE. Through allowing myself to feel this love, over time I gradually regained my inner balance once again.

In our humanity, we experience the loss, the pain and the separation when a loved one passes away. However, if we can open our hearts and minds to the possibility that life is eternal and that 'death' is a time when our loved ones are reborn into the fullness of their souls, then we may be able to be happy for them. As a consequence, we may be able to hold a joyous celebration for our loved ones, even though it is painful to be temporarily separated from them in this physical plane.

From my NDE, I believe that after we 'die' our souls move beyond the restrictions of our human frailties and physical constraints. As a consequence, it is possible to receive the soul's true essence in a deeper, more permanent way. If we can become still enough, we may be able to connect with the real presence and feel a light, joyful, nurturing spirit because our souls' essence can never be destroyed or taken away. I discuss this further in parts 2 and 3 of this book.

I realise that I was blessed to have a loving relationship with my parents, so my main emotion was grief at their loss. However, for many people the death of a family member can bring up a complex array of emotions, depending on the relationship while the parent was alive. These emotions can range from righteous anger, resentment, guilt, relief, furious rage, downright injustice to a whole plethora of other feelings. If you are experiencing these emotions, whatever you feel, please be gentle with yourself and honour your truth. 'E-motions' are supposed to flow, change and hopefully assist with guiding you in the direction of healing.

By early March 2011, after allowing myself to rest and recuperate, I knew that it was time to try to get back to living a normal life again, so I flew to the United States. When I returned to New York, my dear friend Christine Ranck kindly invited me to stay with her once again, on the Upper West Side of Manhattan. The doorman, Jay, smiled when he saw me getting out of the cab with my bags. 'Hey, Róisín, welcome home!'

It really did feel great to be back even though I was emotionally raw. Christine gave me a safe haven to heal my broken heart. I will always be grateful to her. With a combination of humour and compassion, she lifted my spirits and really understood how I felt. She encouraged me to keep going whenever I doubted myself and wondered how it would all come together. Christine is a trauma therapist specialising in Eye Movement Desensitisation and Reprocessing (EMDR), which is a powerful method of accessing and releasing deep emotions in order to live a more balanced life.[23]

While staying with Christine, I had a few sessions with her which enabled me to deal with my grief at the root cause level. With her assistance, I saw the internal conflict between life and death. Christine helped me to see the pattern of believing that I should never have been born, how I had almost exited from this life through the CFS and NDE, and how it was challenging to stay here after my parents' deaths.

I had always believed that I was a 'surprise' for my family, and that I should never have been born. I have known several people over the years who also felt that they were 'surprises' for their parents. There were those who were born to single parents, or before their parents were married, or those who arrived well after their parents thought their family was complete. I realised that I had the choice to let all these distorted and painful human perceptions and beliefs go, no matter how instilled they were in my mind. It was not only my choice, it was my responsibility to create my own life at a deeper soul level. Christine and I worked on healing these feelings by acknowledging and then releasing these early childhood beliefs.

Slowly, I learned to regain my sense of trust. Trust in a Divine presence. Trust in life. Trust in my ability to discern other people clearly. Trust in myself to be able to move forward in life with the guidance of my soul. The synchronicities that ensued gave me the reassurance to continue on, guiding me to fully embrace my soul's truth.

Throughout this period of my life, I kept my steady focus on aligning spiritually, mentally, emotionally and physically through feeling love in my heart and reconnecting with the pure love of Universal Consciousness. I repeated, *'I feel love and radiate light'* quietly in my mind like a mantra, until I shifted the beliefs which were so ingrained and opened up to the truth of my soul's perspective. In doing so, I freed myself to create my life anew. The freedom that I felt was astounding as I focused on making the choice to be fully present on earth and to enjoy living life.

I came to understand the importance for each of us to recognise our worth as human beings. We are all equal at a soul level. We have been given this precious gift of life. If we can realise that we are all physical expressions of the pure love of Universal Consciousness, then we can allow ourselves to receive this Divine guidance to feel and experience this unconditional love in our lives.

During my NDE I discovered that 'Heaven' is a state of being that lies within each and every one of us. Through connecting with this powerful light we can create joy in our everyday lives, even during the most challenging times, because our deepest truth is: we are pure love and always one with the eternal light.

❖ ❖ ❖

During that sojourn in New York, I attended an annual fundraiser which Irish hotelier John Fitzpatrick organised for an Irish children's charity. While I was at the event, I met professional golfer and Ryder Cup winner Christy O'Connor Jnr. The artwork I had donated was being auctioned and I could hear the compère calling out Christy's name. He was bidding on the art and won the piece. I had never met him before so after the auction was over, I introduced myself. He smiled as he said, 'There's healing energy in this art, isn't there?' I nodded. During the conversation with Christy, I learned that he had known both my father and uncle, as they were both great golfers in their heyday. I felt that this was Dad working from the Higher Realms and it was a message that he was with me, supporting me all the way.

Serendipitously, on 19 October 2011, exactly one year on from the day I was told my father was going to die and I had ended my marriage, the opening reception for my solo art exhibition was held at the Consulate General of Ireland, on Park Avenue in New York. It is amazing how we can go from the depths of grief and slowly but surely, by trusting in Divine Power, we can gradually rebuild our lives and come to a place where there is hope and life is worth living again. I dedicated the exhibition to the memory of my parents, for their light to continue to shine.

By a strange quirk of fate, the following year on the second anniversary of Dad's passing, the gentleman who had shared a room with Dad in the hospital came into the family shop on Grafton Street in Dublin. Although he had not been in touch with our family at all in the intervening period of time, when he spoke with one of the members of staff he said that he felt that he had been guided to come in that day. When she explained that it was Dad's anniversary, he seemed to smile knowingly, as if he had guessed who had sent him.

A couple of weeks later, in December 2012, two years after I had experienced so much loss in my life, I was given the opportunity to see how much I had healed over that period of time. While I was in Washington D.C. celebrating Christmas with friends, the photograph on the calendar in my friend's kitchen caught my attention. I stared at the image, hardly believing my eyes. To my amazement, I found myself looking at a panoramic photograph of .Howth. This image was taken on the grounds of Howth Castle, during the rare snap of snowy weather we had experienced in Ireland, at the end of 2010!

This was the time when I had hiked every day on those grounds, past the dolmen, through the forest and fields over to my parents' grave. Day after day during the big freeze, I walked on this trail over the icy snow, as I felt it crunching beneath my feet. The cold air dried my tears, as the bright sunlight illuminated the path, refracting light and hope. I listened to the hushed silence that surrounded me in order to tap into the stillness within my own heart.

When I was grieving the loss of my parents and marriage, two years previously, it had been difficult to imagine ever being happy again at Christmas. Yet, there I found myself, looking at that same image while I was among great friends and enjoying all the festivities and laughing once again. Life was worth living. Firmly grounded in my soul's loving light, the silent hope for peace and joy that I had been willing to embrace, moment to moment, had over time become a reality.

CHAPTER 7

GIFT OF LEARNING

EXPLORING LIGHT IN SCIENCE, ANCIENT IRISH MYTHS AND MEGALITHIC MONUMENTS

I feel blessed to have survived the brain haemorrhage. And, I see every day as a gift, because it is a gift simply to be alive. Experiencing an NDE has, paradoxically, given me complete freedom to live life because I have no fear of dying. My only fear now would be of not fully living and sharing the beauty of the eternal light.

After my NDE, I felt a yearning from deep within, to try to comprehend what I had experienced. I deliberately chose not to read the accounts of other near death experiencers because I wanted to remain clear in my own personal experience. Instead, I found myself drawn to learn more about physics, astronomy, world religions and cultures, ancient Irish legends and the megalithic sites of Ireland in the search for a deeper meaning of life. [25]

Physics

I researched physics in an attempt to gain a scientific perspective and an intellectual explanation for what I had experienced during my NDE. After speaking with a friend of mine who is a science teacher, and my cousin's husband, a lecturer in physics at Cambridge University, I gained a deeper understanding of interconnectivity within the universe.

I learned that everything existing within the universe, at a sub-atomic level, consists of energy in motion, and this energy is in relationship with everything else. If we could look at our bodies with the eyes of a physicist, we would see innumerable particles, atoms, electrons and quarks, whizzing around a vast, empty space. Many of the subatomic particles consist mostly of space and are vibrating with the pure potential of infinite energy. Thus, everything in this physical world is in fact not as solid as it appears, and the intangible is in many ways actually more real. This was my feeling during the NDE, when the boundlessness of the experience was more vivid and alive than the tangible 'reality' of this physical world.

I also learned that quantum physics explains how there are innumerable possibilities. So it is possible that 'I', the observer, am not solely my body, brain or mind, but a form of consciousness, part of the infinity of consciousness. During my NDE, I experienced the oneness of consciousness when I was out of my body, yet still fully alive in a non-physical form.

I also gained an understanding that physics explains how energy can never be eradicated; it simply transforms. Energy cannot be created or destroyed; it can only be changed from one form to another. This was also my experience during my NDE when I gained a new awareness of life and death – we still exist after we 'die', by transforming into a different form of energy. This is an incredibly humbling experience but also a great realisation that this vast expanse of energy can be consciously tapped into at any moment in time. It is available to everyone, all of the time, because we are all pure energy and part of this infinity.

Ironically, I learned that the more I tried to intellectually understand and define my experience during my NDE, the further I seemed to distance myself from the feelings of what I had experienced. I understood that faith and trust were required to stay connected with my soul's deepest truth: faith to choose the feeling of love in my heart over the rational understanding of my brain, faith to select harmony with my soul over comprehension in my mind, and faith to make the feeling of oneness and unity with everything a priority over the duality in this world.

Astronomy
In addition to learning about the sub-atomic energy of physics, I took a course in astronomy to try to develop a framework for understanding the infinity of the physical universe. It is impossible to truly grasp the scale of our

known universe. When we start to see that we are tiny specks on a planet in a solar system that is but a tiny speck of the much grander Milky Way, itself a tiny speck in the infinity of the innumerable galaxies in the known universe, then we begin to open up to the possibilities of life. By looking through this magnified lens, life comes clearly into focus.

One day when I was studying this course, I happened to see two powerful images in a *National Geographic* magazine – one of the vast beauty of the Milky Way and the other of the intricate detail of our DNA. The article discussed the similarity between the pattern of the two images. When I looked closely at the photographs, I was intrigued to see that the shape of the Milky Way seemed to be very similar in design to the cross-section of our DNA. This came to mean something profound for me – symbolising the theme of unity and oneness throughout everything in this physical realm.

The same double-spiral configuration appears to exist at both the macro level of the universe and the micro level of our DNA. So not only are we physically made from the stellar ash, the same elements as the stars in the sky – carbon, oxygen, nitrogen, phosphorous, sulphur etc. – but a similar design seems to be replicated in the structure of our cells. I created an artwork (the design on the cover of this book) as an artistic representation of the Whirlpool/DNA pattern, to symbolise this theme of unity.

Darkness and Light in World Cultures and Religions
Many spiritual traditions and world mythologies have

tried to explain the mysteries of the universe. The concept of creation, with darkness preceding the light, resonates deep in the psyche with people of various cultures and ethnic backgrounds around the planet, from the northern to the southern hemispheres.

This concept is also at the core of many religions such as the Eastern Hindu faith with the *Diwali* (Festival of Lights) representing the victory of light over darkness. In Islam it is portrayed in the Koran: 'Praise be to Allah, Who created the heavens and the earth, and made darkness and light' (Surat Al-Anaam). And it is also shared in Western religious texts, including the Bible: 'And God said, Let there be light; and there was light.'[24]

Similarly, in old Irish tradition, the dark precedes the light. This is shown by the division of the year into two halves. The first half of the year commences in the dark of winter at *Samhain* (pronounced *sow-en*), which marks the Celtic New Year.

The second half of the year commences in the light of the summer with the festival of *Bealtaine* (pronounced *bel-tin-e*), which takes place at the beginning of May. The interconnectedness of dark/death and light/life form an integrated cycle within the ever-changing, evolving, eternal spiral of life.

After my NDE, I realised that regular themes in our old Irish myths, and the recurrent solar phenomena at many of the megalithic monuments, appeared to illustrate the juxtaposition of light and darkness. I knew that there was a powerful connection between the energy I had experienced during my NDE and the profound wisdom of Irish tradition. It was fascinating to learn just how much the ancient Irish people seemed to have revered light as it appears to be one of the fundamental tenets of our legends, Neolithic architecture and even pre-Celtic art.

> *Many times man lives and dies*
> *Between his two eternities,*
> *That of race and that of soul,*
> *And ancient Ireland knew it all.*
> From 'Under Ben Bulben' by W.B. Yeats[26]

Legends and Megalithic Monuments of Ancient Ireland

Since these legends are based on an oral tradition of story-telling, I decided that one of the best ways to learn about these tales and discover their contemporary relevance was to hear them first-hand. I embarked on a journey to the Bard School on Clare Island, which is located off the west coast of Ireland at the entrance of Clew Bay. Every summer people from all around the world gather on Clare Island to explore these tales through delving into the dreamlike and colourful world of Irish myth.[27]

Mid-summer on the west coast of Ireland, we huddled together at the harbour of Roonagh Quay, waiting for the ferry to take us on the 20-minute ride from the mainland to Clare Island. The gusts of wind swirled around us, with sheets of rain drenching us as they lashed sideways, covering our clothes in a moist spray.

'This place would be gorgeous in the summer,' a Dubliner exclaimed.

To which he received a quick retort from a local man, 'Sure, 'tis the middle of the summer now, lad. You're goin' to an island off the west of Ireland, not the feckin' Caribbean!'

We all laughed as we boarded the boat.

Keeping my eyes firmly focused in a steady gaze on the island on the horizon as the squall surged around us, I noticed that the island kept appearing and disappearing in a silvery haze. The organiser of the course smiled. 'Your journey is beginning now. We are starting to enter into the "Otherworld". As in the voyages of Bran, Mael Dúin and Oisín, we are travelling across the seas to a place where the visible becomes invisible and everything comes joyously to life.' After studying the Irish myths in books, it was now time to open my heart for the elusive spirit of the stories to magically appear before my eyes.

Over the next few days we learned about the oldest Irish legends, the foundation myths of Ireland. The first people to arrive on Irish shores were led by a woman, Ceasair, and her partner Fionntan.

In this poetic rendition of the history of Ireland, Ceasair's tribe was succeeded by waves of peoples who also landed on Irish shores, the Partholonians, Nemedians, Fomorians, the Fir Bolg and then the *Tuatha Dé Danann* (pronounced *too-ha day dan-an*), or 'People of the Goddess Danu', referred to in shorter form as the *Tuatha Dé*.[28]

The *Tuatha Dé* were the principal otherworldly race in Irish literary myth. These supernatural and immortal deities were known by some modern scholars [. . .] 'Lords of light and life', 'Gods of life and light' a[nd] 'Ever-Living Ones'.[29]

When we began retelling the stories of the light-filled *Tuatha Dé*, by serendipity, the clouds lifted and the light from the sun's rays shone on Clare Island. This light stayed with us for the next week, from the early sunrise until it dipped behind the ridgeline around 10.30 p.m. In the distant shore, the low-lying mountains of Achill and Achillbeg Islands formed a silhouette of a reclining goddess. As dusk encroached, the wisps of cloud stratifying over the land delicately bathed her in a light, vaporous haze of orange and lilac hue.

While lying on the grass, feeling at one with the beauty of nature, my mind wandered. It was easy to understand how the prehistoric peoples may have believed in the 'People of the goddess Danu', *Tuatha Dé*. Surrounded by such spectacular scenery, it was possible to sense the unbounded spirit which is at the foundation of this ancient lore.

In these legends, Ireland was populated by the *Tuatha Dé*, and when the land was invaded by the Milesians, the shimmering light-filled *Tuatha Dé* retreated underground. They went below the surface at sacred places in Ireland, such as the megalithic monument at Newgrange, where according to legend they still live in peace in these 'Otherworlds'.

In Irish lore, there are many 'Otherworlds' where these mystical beings live, such as 'The Land of Eternal

Youth', 'The Land of the Living' and 'The Plain of Joy', a delightful and pleasurable paradise.[30] In these 'Otherworlds', the *Tuatha Dé* live for eternity in peace and harmony. There are numerous myths about these radiant beings having extraordinary powers and phenomenal energy. They have great abilities of insight and knowing and are skilfully able to transform their own energy to manifest changes in the world around them.

As a young child, I remember listening to these legends with awe, as they sparked my furtive imagination. However, as I grew older, that sense of wonder turned to incredulity. Now, as an adult, having experienced an NDE, I have a greater appreciation and understanding of these traditional stories. I realise their full value and respect their message. They appear to beautifully illustrate the infinite Divine Wisdom that is available to us all. This all-encompassing, eternal, light-filled energy is our real essence and deepest truth.

During my NDE, I learned that we are all created from pure energy. I believe now that we are beings created from eternal light, and that we can change our lives and transform to become increasingly light-filled. So the shimmering and shape-shifting beings of light, *Tuatha Dé*, may not be as illusory a concept as I had thought in my teenage years. These revered legends show us that we have the ability to make choices in our lives. When we decide to tap into the Universal Consciousness that is available to us all, we can literally shift our energy and become wiser, gaining greater insights and knowledge.

From my NDE experience, I also learned that the

'Otherworld' really does exist after we face so-called death. Our souls or spirits continue to exist, just in another form, beyond any constraints of time or space. The feelings of blissful love, joy, harmony and peace are all-pervasive in the 'Otherworld' – the eternal realm beyond what our human senses can see.

This tradition, like those of many other ancient cultures, brings this wisdom to life. Even if it appears to be invisible to our naked human eye, we are given a deeper insight and clarity of vision to see an illuminated way for us to journey on this path of life. 'Sight in you will be pure wonder ... sight in you will be more visionary than vision.'[31]

However, it appears that in some of the written texts the status of the *Tuatha Dé* deities gradually diminished over the centuries. They were demoted from omniscient divinity to semi-divinity. Even Lugh, the gifted *Tuatha Dé* god, the 'Shining One' and 'Master of All Arts', may have been relegated to the role of the mischievous, trickster leprechaun.[32]

Nonetheless, the *Tuatha Dé* remained bound up in the landscape. Many of the megalithic monuments, also known as Neolithic mounds, which are visible throughout the Irish countryside, were considered to be the dwelling places of the *Tuatha Dé* and, as such, portals to the 'Otherworld'. Hence, the *Tuatha Dé* were referred to as the 'people of the Otherworld mounds', the 'earthly gods' and *sídh*.[33]

The Neolithic mounds which are dotted around the countryside, still guard the secrets of our ancient past, keeping the memory of the eternal light alive. Just as the light is kept alive in the myths, though they may change, this light is also enshrined in these large stone monuments.

When sunlight penetrates into the depths of these Neolithic mounds at sunrise or sunset, it may be seen to represent a life-force of light that can never be extinguished. This spark of eternal light continues to burn brightly, inspiring and igniting our deepest souls' yearnings. There is an elusive energy which defies empirical description at these ancient sites. And, when struck by solar phenomena in the form of rays of sunlight, megaliths become breathtakingly beautiful.

I invite you to take a journey with me to some of these megalithic monuments situated in the Boyne Valley in County Meath, north-west of Dublin. Built by our Neolithic ancestors over 5,000 years ago, they awaken within us a sense of awe at their pioneering and indomitable spirit which has transcended the millennia. Through their legacy of monuments, this highly sophisticated race continues to gently remind us of the powerful nature of the light.

Newgrange is the most famous of these Neolithic sites in Ireland. This architectural feat predates both Stonehenge in Britain and the pyramids in Egypt. It consists of a huge stone mound, which has a passageway leading to an interior chamber. For the days around the time of the winter solstice in December, when the sun is lowest in the sky and rises at dawn, the golden sunlight travels through the entrance, along the passageway, to illuminate the chamber at the rear. This is the only time during the year when the sunlight reaches deep into the recesses of the chamber. When this occurs, a beautiful triple-spiral symbol which is carved out from stone is brought brilliantly to light. It heralds the beginning of the celebrated ascension of the sun into the sky, until it begins to fall again at the summer solstice.

While standing in the cavernous space of the inner chamber at Newgrange, when the winter solstice phenomenon is simulated with a golden beam of light illuminating the entire space, one feels a sense of sacredness and power surrounding the annual ritual of light. Over five millennia ago, at this exact location, our ancestors also stood beneath the same conical, corbelled roof, experiencing the aura of peace that pervades this site. This is not the macabre experience of a mausoleum, but instead an inspiring, invigorating sense of hopefulness – a portal to the 'Otherworld', a doorway to the afterlife, and a light-filled path to eternity.

All the memories of my NDE flood back into my mind. Immersed once again in the experience of moving from the world of physical constraints into the realm of limitless spiritual freedom, shifting from the depths of darkness to the warmth of the light, transforming from the finite view of mortality to the perspective of infinite life and love, I feel the bliss, the beautiful, boundless, unconditionally loving bliss.

In the focused beam of light from without, the secrets concealed within the Neolithic chamber are brought to life. Standing on the same hallowed ground within the chamber at Newgrange, where the ancient builders of this site stood millennia earlier, a quiet stillness seems to permeate up from the depths of the earth below. We are given an opportunity for our hearts to beat to the same ancestral drum, as we recognise the importance of our existence within the grander design of unity with all that exists.

Just as the return of the sacred light at the winter solstice is hailed at Newgrange with the rising sun at dawn, the setting sun is celebrated at another location, Dowth.[34] Dowth, which in Irish (*Dubhadh*) means darkness, is located over a mile away (1.2 miles) from Newgrange. Around the period of the winter solstice, light from the setting sun enters into the chamber located at this site, thus completing the cycle between the light and darkness. During the winter months from October through to February, the light of the setting sun entering the shorter passageway at Dowth changes colour in a similar manner to those which I experienced during my NDE. In the early winter months we can observe the bright beam change to a warm yellow, then become a golden-pink around the time of the solstice, and transform to a rich honey gold and eventually to a white light by February.[35]

After having experienced an NDE, these Neolithic sites hold a very special place in my heart. They seem to gently lure me in to taking a journey to reconnect with the eternal light, where the material and non-material worlds meld into one. Whenever I visit the region of the Boyne Valley, I feel myself instinctively tuning in to the high vibrations of these sites. I experience a similar feeling to that which I experienced as a child at the dolmen in Howth – the distinctive, barely audible whisper, the feeling of returning 'home' and the power of connecting with something so mysterious yet fully comprehensible in a language which is beyond words.

I believe that these Neolithic sites may represent the transition of life and death and how ultimately life, just like this light, can never be extinguished. At times this light may disappear and seem as if it has gone. However, this is only an illusion. This light, like life, is eternal and always exists as beautiful, brilliant and bright as ever.

The Neolithic monuments and ancient tales of Ireland evoke our souls' highest potential and deepest truth. The questions are: are we ready to reconnect with such archetypes as the *Tuatha Dé*, the 'Gods of life and light'? Do we have the courage to bring the wisdom out from the depths of the sacred stone sites and back into our living hearts? Are we willing to embrace the blissful love, joy, peace and beauty of the 'Otherworlds', to live with this sense of wonder and joy in our everyday lives? Are we willing to grasp the opportunity to share the harmonious beauty of the eternal light and leave an inspiring legacy for the generations who will live 50 centuries from now?

A more in-depth description of my journey discovering the eternal light in Irish heritage and its relevance in our modern lives will be shared in my next book, *Eternal Light: Solas Síoraí*.

I was amazed to find every aspect of my NDE described in our myths. It was astounding for me to find both the

CHAPTER 8

GIFT OF LIFE NOW

One year after meeting Dr Greyson, I returned to see him again at the University of Virginia in Charlottesville. Although we had remained in contact during the year and he knew about some of my discoveries, it was still a joy to meet in person once again. It felt like a reunion of kindred spirits.

I thanked him for encouraging me to venture on this path of grounding my NDE in my Irish heritage. 'You will never guess what I discovered,' I said.

Dr Greyson looked at me inquisitively, enthusiastic to hear what I was about to share.

'A common phrase for saying "May you rest in peace" in Gaelic is *solas síoraí*, which literally means the "eternal light" in English. This beautifully illustrates the interconnectivity of light between the realms of life and death.'

'Róisín, this is wonderful,' he replied.

We continued to speak together for a few hours as I relayed all my findings and he probed deeper, with each question building on the previous one. I shared what I had learned about this ancient culture and how this research brought me to a deeper, more profound understanding when I discovered how the thread of eternal light wove seamlessly through the Neolithic sites in Ireland, ancient Irish tales and my experience during my NDE. Dr Greyson was delighted. 'This is way beyond what I imagined you would find,' he said.

As we continued chatting, while he showed me around his research facilities at the university, I spoke in more depth about how my whole perspective of life had changed radically since my NDE. I now interpret life differently. I am aware that everything and everyone is, at a fundamental level, a form of light, a form of energy, so much so that I have changed my life to become a visual artist to express this new interpretation and share the beauty of this light.

Dr Greyson kindly spent the afternoon with me. I loved listening to him as he shared his research, retelling stories and anecdotes about his findings over the past four decades. He has amassed a depth of understanding and comprehension of life and consciousness, yet he has such a humble and unassuming presence. As I was leaving I asked Dr Greyson how I could assist him with his work.

He replied, 'Publish your books, Róisín. People need to hear about the eternal light – *solas síoraí* – and know that everyone has the ability to be able to feel, experience and live with this love as part of our everyday lives. Share with people your understanding that there is no death *per se* but each one of us is part of an ever-changing, evolving form of consciousness – one of pure love.'

My Life Now

I still live in my coastal home, just south of County Dublin. Blessed to enjoy great health now, I certainly don't take it for granted anymore. My journey also continues as an artist, sharing my work as Artist of the Light. I feel fortunate that my artworks are now on public display in places such as the National Concert Hall in Dublin city, the Irish-American Heritage Museum in upstate New York and Glucksman Ireland House, the Department of Irish Studies at New York University. This art is also on permanent display at the Anam Cara Gallery in Greenwich, Connecticut where the owner Patti Kane embodies the light of the *Tuatha Dé* and radiates this so beautifully in her gallery. John Fitzpatrick also kindly shows my art at his Fitzpatrick's Grand Central Hotel in Manhattan. Though not related, as many people assume we are given that we both share the same surname, John has always encouraged me and supported my work.

I have recently completed a corporate commission of seven artworks for, an international biotechnology company whose European headquarters are in Dunboyne, near the Boyne Valley. It was a joy to create these artworks. Inspired by designs from Newgrange and the other megalithic monuments of this region, these artworks bring this ancient wisdom to light. They reflect how the innovation of our ancestors over five millennia ago continues into modern times with the pioneering work of this successful company.

My journey with the light also continues, with numerous bleary-eyed, pre-dawn ventures out in the darkness, driving through the Irish countryside hoping to catch a glimpse of the early-morning sun entering some of the Neolithic mounds.

What is the next step on this journey? I honestly don't know but I trust that wherever it brings me I will always be guided by my soul and Universal Consciousness. I hope to be able to share this loving light in a way that it inspires people to tap into their own inner light, for each and every one of us is always part of the eternal light.

PART 2

INSIGHTS FROM MY
NEAR DEATH EXPERIENCE:
FOR LIVING AND LOVING
YOUR LIFE

*Look at every path closely and deliberately, then ask this
crucial question: does this path have a heart?
If it does, then the path is good. If it doesn't,
then it is of no use to us.*
Carlos Castaneda

The most precious gift that you can give to yourself is the realisation that you are pure love. You are – at your very core, essence, deepest truth – a physical expression of Universal Consciousness which is pure love.

Many of us spend so much of our time either running away from ourselves or simply trying to come to peace with ourselves that we remain unaware of this essential truth. As a consequence, the idea of actually experiencing such love in our daily lives may seem almost impossible.

What would happen if we chose to give ourselves a break and lighten up? Instead of spending so much time judging ourselves, berating ourselves for not attaining ridiculously high standards (usually self-imposed), or trampling on our own dreams in order to please other people's expectations of who we ought to be: *what would happen if we chose to open up to feeling this love in our daily lives?*

By opening up to the possibility that all the love we seek is within, we can begin to understand that it is not necessary for us to do or achieve anything, or to change ourselves in any way in order to become worthy of experiencing this love. We are worthy simply by being physical expressions of the unconditional love of Universal Consciousness. This infinite Source of pure love lies within us and all around us. If we can shift our awareness to recognise this truth, then we can naturally tap into this unconditional love. By making this choice, we become able to radiate this love outwards, touching everyone in our lives.

The realisation of self-love is the key to creating our most inspired and joyous lives.

Love, cherish and adore ourselves. Really? YES! Initially, it can feel strange and even alien as a concept to love ourselves because this is not the way we are normally brought up in society. But this is not a narcissistic, ego-driven, selfish love seeking to self-aggrandise at the expense of others, or to disempower anyone in any way. Quite the opposite: it is a recognition that love is our real essence. By allowing ourselves to let go of the false beliefs that block the expression of this love, we naturally become aligned with the pure love of Universal Consciousness.

If we choose to live life in a more compassionate and heart-centred way, as opposed to the often stressful and frustrating mind-focused manner to which we have become accustomed in modern society, this can have huge benefits in all areas of our lives. In addition to the well-documented improvements in our long-term health and greater mental clarity, not only do we feel and experience more love in our own lives, we also radiate this love outwards, affecting everyone we meet.

This is why the relationship with yourself is by far the most important relationship in your life. By allowing yourself to feel love, you create the opportunity to align – spiritually, mentally, emotionally and physically – with your soul to receive the pure love of Universal Consciousness. By choosing to reconnect with this love you gain mastery over your own life. And, the more you allow this love to flow into your life, the more you can share this love with others.

Your unconditionally loving presence is the most precious gift that you can give to everyone you meet in life. This may inspire others, consciously or unconsciously, to reconnect with the love of Universal Consciousness which is available to us all.

So if you decide that you would like to live a more empowered life, how can you feel this love and tap into this infinite world of possibilities if you have not experienced this yourself through an NDE, or a similar spiritual awakening?

I am not a scientist or a theologian; what I can share though are some insights I gleaned from my wonderful life-changing NDE which radically altered my whole perspective on life and death. I wish to share this with you so that, if you choose, you may ask deeper questions examining your perception of 'reality', in particular where scientific research intersects with spiritual wisdom. I don't have the answers; however, through asking thought-provoking questions, perhaps together we can open our minds and hearts to see if we can be inspired to create better lives.

I hope this section of the book may encourage you to become more inquisitive about life. You may wish to experiment with some of the ideas. You may become increasingly curious and ask more reflective questions about who you really are and what life is all about. *What is your purpose? What is the universe? Is there a Divine Power with which we co-create this 'reality'?* If you give yourself the freedom to be open to the possibility of new answers, the responses may astound you.

As you ask more questions, you may find more answers, and as a result feel a greater sense of empowerment and loving connection with your soul and Universal Consciousness. You may also find that many areas of your life flow in more joyous and inspired ways. There is no one-way approach to life. There are an infinite number of possibilities from which to choose. Only you can determine the best path for your life.

Since my NDE, I know for certain that there is so much more to life than I will ever be able to fully comprehend with this tiny brain of mine. Like trying to catch a firefly – as soon as it is grasped, the light becomes extinguished and all the mystical beauty vanishes. In a similar manner during my NDE, when I was surrounded by what felt like billions of fireflies, by surrendering and not trying to control the situation, I opened up to the experience that followed. I learned that consciousness is far greater than the brain or the mind. It is an enigma. It cannot be restricted or confined. I now have great reverence and respect for Universal Consciousness and the power of Divine Wisdom, and I gently flow in the direction it guides me.

Although I am always open to gain a deeper understanding in my mind, I learned that the most important answers invariably come from my heart. During my NDE, the answer to every question that I asked was always the same: *love, pure, unconditional, heart-warming, boundless love.* The love I experienced during my NDE was more real than anything I have ever felt in the physical realm. It makes this tangible world seem like a hazy dream by comparison.

In the following section, I share a few ideas based on my experience during the NDE. Some of the suggestions may resonate well with you, and others less so. If you wish, please select those which work for you. You may find some of them useful in different situations or at various stages during your life.

I wish to share in this section of the book the loving, eternal light which is available, here and now, for everyone. When I merged and became one with this during my NDE, I realised that everything exists as pure energy before it becomes thought or word or takes physical form. This is why it is so important to be aware of the thoughts that we think, words that we say and actions that we take, because they mould this energy into shape.

When we can overcome our fears, we can live life with love in our hearts, insight from our souls and guidance from Divine Wisdom. When we are willing to seek this guidance, then our daily lives can be transformed from being ordinary to becoming extraordinary.

1. Reconnect With Your Soul's True Essence

2. Face Death and Embrace Life

3. Live Your Life Now

4. Release Fear and Choose Love

5. Integrate Your Whole Self

6. Connect with the Love in Your Heart and Universal Consciousness – SSSSSH Technique

1) RECONNECT WITH YOUR SOUL'S TRUE ESSENCE

Every great dream begins with a dreamer.
Harriet Tubman

There are numerous ways of connecting with your soul and Universal Consciousness. Many people have experienced a defining moment or flash of Divine intervention. For some people, it may be a profound dream, an amazing serendipity, or the experience of a powerful *déjà vu*. For others, it can occur around the birth of a child, the death of a loved one, or from sensing the presence of someone dear who has passed over. These are the moments of clarity, when we see through the illusory veil of this material realm. People often experience these as a feeling of deep inner peace, a serene tranquillity or an intense love. This is our true nature and the essence of who we really are.

Take a few moments to remember such times in your own life. If they come back into your mind, sit quietly with them, try to re-experience all the feelings and emotions. By consciously choosing to reconnect with these moments again and again, you can reconnect with your soul's truth.

2) FACE DEATH AND EMBRACE LIFE

Every day, think as you wake up, today I am fortunate to be alive, I have a precious human life, I am not going to waste it. I am going to use all my energies to develop myself, to expand my heart out to others.
Dalai Lama

In Western society, we rarely discuss death. As a consequence, we avoid looking at our own mortality, unless we are forced to do so. Like most people, I spent a lot of time avoiding the one absolute certainty in life, which is death. I ran around keeping myself busy because, at a deeper level throughout my teens and up until my mid-twenties, I had absolutely no belief in the existence of anything beyond the physical realm. There is no way that I would have ever faced the fear voluntarily. However, through experiencing CFS and then most particularly my NDE, I have embraced this fear of death. Ironically, it has given me the freedom to truly live my best life.

One of the wisest people I know lives every day with the courage to face his mortality. He often says, 'Sure why wouldn't I, the worms are winking up at me. Every day that I am above ground and not below is a gift. It's a joy to be alive.'

It is true that when we have the courage to face our mortality, we learn to recognise every day as a valuable gift of life. We may also learn to cope with death, by possibly seeing it as a transition to the eternal light. This may help us to face not only our own death but also to assist others by focusing on the needs of the dying person and the needs of those left behind in the throes of grief.

If you wish, you can face this fear of death now and possibly shift your perspective to view life as part of the loving, eternal light. By freeing yourself of this fear, you create the opportunity *to live your greatest life and full potential right now*. You may alter the trajectory of your life, positively influencing not only your own life but also the lives of everyone you touch in your lifetime.

3) LIVE YOUR LIFE NOW

It is astonishing to say that after a lifetime of studying the human condition, all I can say is to try to be a little bit more kind.

Aldous Huxley (said on his deathbed)

Each one of us is a form of energy, temporarily residing in a physical body. If you have ever witnessed a person dying, at one moment the person you know and love is physically here, in this material realm; in the next, indiscernible moment, you are standing by a lifeless corpse. What is the difference? That spark of light, vital force, life energy, whatever you wish to call it, the intangible, untouchable, unreachable and unfathomable; yet this is the difference between life and death.

If I learned one thing from my NDE it is that all that matters in life is to love and be loved. When we pass over to the 'other side' we merge with this love and realise, 'Aha, so that's what life was all about!' Having been given a glimpse of what lies ahead after 'death', I feel fortunate to have been given another chance to come back and truly live life. If it feels right for you, I encourage you to take a look at your life now.

We often hear people speak of their 'bucket list', the sights they would like to see and adventures they would like to have in the world before they die. Instead of a 'bucket list', filled with travels and expeditions, what if we imagine an inner journey or quest, that is a 'quest-ion list' for journeying into our hearts?

'Quest-ion' for you: imagine if you reviewed who you want to be before you die. This could have a huge impact on how you choose to live the rest of your life.

Try visualising yourself dying now, not on your deathbed years in the future. In this present moment, right now, ask yourself the question: *am I truly living my best life?*

Rather than a question of what you want to do, or where you want to go or what you want to see, ask yourself: are you living the life you were born to live? Are you being the person your soul is guiding you to be?

Give yourself the opportunity to look at every aspect of what you are currently creating by taking the time to examine your life from this perspective. What energy are you emitting? Are you coming from love and sharing freely from the heart, or are you coming from fear, letting limiting thoughts and beliefs rule and constrain your life and the lives of those around you?

As you take a look at all areas of your life, see what you are creating. What are your relationships like with your family, friends, neighbours, co-workers and community? What changes can you make to live a more loving life? What way are you prioritising your time and energy? Also, observe the quality of your interactions. How could you be more present with an open heart and mind in every aspect of your life?

When you stand back and observe, you may find that, ultimately, the only issue of any value is whether you are being a loving person and sharing this love with people in a way that enriches their lives. When you stop to take a clear look at life and death, everything that is superficial or insignificant falls by the wayside as clarity of insight is gained. Most people realise that all that really matters is giving and receiving love.

I was blessed to have the experience of looking death straight in the eye. It has given me a second chance at life. All that truly counts for me is to integrate with my soul and share this love. After my NDE, I reorganised my priorities on how I wished to live my life moving forward. I now choose to surround myself with people who are also taking responsibility for their lives and what they share in this world. As well as giving thanks for everyone and everything that contributes to my life in a positive way, I also give gratitude for the growth opportunities which I would not intentionally have chosen, and trust me, there are many of those too. This gratitude then expands and multiplies exponentially.

The gift from your own 'quest-ion list' is that you can reflect upon all aspects of your life without having to go through a spiritual crisis. You can see if you are truly living the life for which you were born. By making the necessary changes now, as opposed to postponing them, you can alter the course of the rest of your life. By facing death, you free yourself to fully embrace your life.

If we choose to focus on the past, rationalising our current behaviour patterns and blaming others for the pain in our lives, then that is what we continue to re-create. If we focus on the future, postponing our happiness until expectations are met, then we will never be happy. All of our power exists right here, right now. If we focus on living life from our hearts, we can become empowered. By intentionally deciding to focus on the best option now, in the present moment, we become open to receiving our souls' guidance for creating our future aligned with Universal Consciousness.

4) RELEASE FEAR AND CHOOSE LOVE

I learned that courage was not the absence of fear,
but the triumph over it. The brave man is not he who
does not feel afraid, but he who conquers that fear.
  Nelson Mandela

We do not necessarily have control over everything that happens in our lives. Some Eastern cultures would suggest that events occur as a result of karma, while Western cultures might call this fate. Nonetheless, whatever you decide to call it, we always have the choice as to how we respond to these situations. This is our responsibility.

How we decide to react to circumstances will determine our destinies. Our greatest truth and highest purpose always beckon us, if we become still enough to listen to our souls' guidance, and courageous enough to act on this advice. We each have a unique path. When we tune into our souls' purpose, we can live the life of our dreams. By allowing the love of Universal Consciousness to flow through us on this journey, we can create a better world for ourselves, the societies we live in, and all of humanity.

Life expands if it is lived from a place of love, or contracts if it is lived from a place of fear. The degree to which we separate ourselves from our souls' truths, through fears, negative beliefs, anger and doubts, is the degree to which we distance ourselves from this love. If we choose fear, we disconnect from our highest truth and our lives become smaller and constrained. As the fears take over, our inner light becomes dimmed and our lives contract accordingly.

However, if we choose love, we reconnect with our souls at a deeper level. As our inner light shines more brightly, life expands with boundless possibilities. This contraction or expansion is in direct proportion to the courage a person brings to face their fears and move through the challenges encountered in life. Each time love is chosen over fear, a Divine Power responds, providing more opportunities for an even greater soul connection. The strength to choose love over fear in every situation provides the foundation for living life from our hearts.

5) INTEGRATE YOUR WHOLE SELF

> *The privilege of a lifetime is to become who you truly are.*
> Carl Jung

The most important relationship in your life is your relationship with yourself. If we take the Jungian approach to looking at ourselves, we recognise that we are all capable of everything, from the most heinous crimes to the most selfless acts of bravery. When we shine light with courage and profound love on the parts which we most want to conceal, we bring this shadow to light by acknowledging these aspects of ourselves. We find when we observe these characteristics with the light, by looking through our souls' loving lens, we see that the original thoughts or beliefs from which these characteristics developed were not based on love.

Therefore, whether these thoughts came from society, our cultural or educational systems or our families, the source is irrelevant; all that matters is the question: do these thoughts come from love? If the answer is no, then we have the choice to rise to the challenge and let them go now.

Love is the deepest truth of who we are. Love shows us that fear is an illusion. When we switch the light on, all the darkness and our fears of the darkness disappear. Similarly, when we can see life from our souls' loving perspective, then the illusory fear-based beliefs disappear. However, sometimes these beliefs can be so deep-seated that we think they form part of our identity, or are a fundamental part of our beings. It can be extremely uncomfortable to release them, no matter how destructive they are in our lives.

If we challenge fears by treating ourselves with kindness and compassion, we can not only learn to face but actually embrace these fears and let them go. It is through the moment-to-moment, day-to-day choice to come from our hearts with love, rather than negative, fear-based thoughts that we can liberate ourselves from our fears. On other occasions, leaps of faith are required. By having the courage to stand on the edge and take the flight, we can soar to reach the height of our potential.

Every time you challenge a belief or thought that did not come from love and is therefore untrue, you access and reintegrate another part of your soul. By setting the intention to merge with the highest potential of your soul and continuously challenging your negative beliefs and thoughts, you remove the obstacles that prevent you from creating your best life.

Love and the infinite possibilities of your soul are your real truth. These emerge naturally, when the negative thoughts are released. Thus, by continuously choosing love and light, the energy you emit will be one of love. This is also the frequency which can open new doors in your life, as any barriers rooted in fear are inevitably removed. Once the energy is at this frequency, then the momentum of the energy keeps creating in this direction. By focusing on love, more love manifests in every way.

6) CONNECT WITH THE LOVE IN YOUR HEART AND UNIVERSAL CONSCIOUSNESS

As man thinketh in his heart, so is he.
Proverbs 23:7

Your life can transform in ways you cannot even begin to imagine by connecting with Universal Consciousness and allowing this energy to flow through you. Rather than being led by the tirades of an unconscious mind, you can choose to be gently guided by the love in your heart.

All that is required to live your soul's truth is a willingness to be open to the possibility of the existence of a Higher Consciousness with which we co-create our 'reality'. This wisdom is presented to us throughout our daily lives, continuously providing spiritual guidance. When we listen to our inner voice, which is unique for each of us, we hear messages through our senses, feelings, gut instinct and synchronistic signs. These synchronicities happen automatically when we become aligned with Universal Consciousness because we experience the oneness of flowing with this energy of infinite possibilities.

Going within is one of the most powerful ways of reconnecting with this infinite Source of unconditional love. I must admit, the first time I tried to become still and meditate on 'nothing' I thought to myself, why on earth would I ever want to do this? However, after my NDE, I understood the value of being still. Through stillness, I was able to tap into the silence within, and access the place of 'no-thing'. This is the Source of pure energy, when it is most alive and vibrant, just before it has moulded to manifest into thought or physical form or action.

There are many ways of tapping into this life-force, such as meditation, yoga, silent retreats, connecting with nature, and in the presence of dear family and friends. Another way is through consciously choosing thoughts that align us with this vibration.

The key is to make the decision to let your heart, as opposed to your head, guide you through life.

Below is a simple but effective technique for quickly shifting your energy. In a moment, you can leave the merry-go-round of fear-based thinking and reconnect with the love in your heart. In doing so, you naturally align with the love of Universal Consciousness. By making this choice, those moments can grow into minutes, hours, days, weeks, months and years. From the moment you make that initial choice and then continuously choose to keep the momentum of your energy focused in the new direction, your life can change dramatically. By choosing to feel the love in your heart, you automatically connect with Universal Consciousness.

SSSSSH Technique: Silence to Reconnect with the Love in Your Heart and Universal Consciousness

1. Stop: Stop

2. Still: Become still

3. Slow breathing: Take deep breaths to relax your whole body and mind. If you make sure that your back is straight with your shoulders pulled back and down, this increases your lung capacity and improves the quality of your breathing

4. Smile: This changes the physiology of your body and calms your mind so you begin to feel lighter and more joyful

5. Soul: Set the intention to connect with the pure love of your soul and Universal Consciousness

6. Heart: Gently place the tips of your first two

fingers at your heart in the middle of your chest
as you repeat with words out loud, '*I feel love
and radiate light.*'

Keep breathing slowly, while smiling, as you allow
yourself to experience a beautiful feeling of love at
your heart. Slowly allow this feeling of love to spread
throughout your entire body and beyond.

*At this moment you are connected with the pure love of
your soul and Universal Consciousness.*

The key is to feel the love expanding your heart. In
order to feel this love when you first do this exercise, it
may be helpful to think of someone you love, or a pet
or a favourite place you love to visit, anything which
creates the feeling of love, and then allow this feeling to
grow and permeate your whole body and beyond.

Another way of feeling more love in your heart is to
imagine on each 'in' breath that you are receiving the pure
love of the Universal Consciousness through your heart,
at the centre of your chest. As you breathe 'out', imagine
radiating this pure love of Universal Consciousness back
out into the infinity of the universe from your heart.
Allow yourself to feel your heart area opening up and
expanding.

By consciously reconnecting through your heart to
the pure love of Universal Consciousness, you create the
opportunity to become aligned on all levels – spiritual,
mental, emotional and physical – with the vibration
of pure love. At this higher frequency you allow the
oneness of Universal Consciousness to flow through you

and, as a consequence, you may experience any or all of the following:

- your thought process becomes more focused with greater clarity;

- you become more compassionate towards yourself and everyone in your life;

- you gain a clearer, healthier and broader perspective on all the key issues in your life from relationships, to work and health;

- you experience an inner peace and harmony;

- you open yourself to receiving insights and Divine guidance;

- you experience more serendipities and coincidences in life;

- you gain a greater reverence and awe for the beauty of life.

Through the continuous practice of this simple SSSSSH Technique, it is possible for you to radically transform your life. Constant repetition is the key. Like any form of exercise, you may resist what is in your best interest and find every excuse under the sun to avoid doing this. However, if you continue practising this technique, you may find that you quickly reap the benefits and actually want to continue practising until this becomes second nature to you.

If you are feeling sceptical, I encourage you to be open to the possibility that this could be an effective technique. I will share with you the story of a friend of mine who was initially dubious, but because he was going through a particularly stressful time at work, he decided to give it a try. He told me that he had nothing to lose and potentially everything to gain.

For the next few weeks he repeated this SSSSSH Technique in the mornings and throughout the day whenever it came to mind. Sometimes he really could feel the heart connection and other times he simply could not. Nonetheless, he kept saying, 'I feel love and radiate light,' out loud when he was on his own, or he quietly repeated the words in his mind when he was in the company of others. He continued this practise, while breathing slowly, smiling and touching his heart, knowing that the feeling would return.

Then one day, my friend approached me. 'I am exasperated. I can't figure this out. I felt great for a while and now the more I concentrate on this, for some reason, it's no longer working.'

'Show me what you are doing and let's see,' I replied.

He stared at me, concentrating so hard that his face was almost scowling, with deep furrows embedded in his brow, as he repeated, 'I feel love and radiate light, I feel love and radiate light.'

I mirrored back to him, with an exaggerated frown on my face, in a deep guttural tone, 'I feel love and radiate light,' and I continued, 'Do I honestly look like I'm feelin' da lurve?'

He burst out laughing. 'Ah, so I am to smile and allow myself to *feel* love.'

'Yes, that's it! Even if you can only feel a bit quieter and calmer at the beginning, the more you let go and allow yourself to become lighter in mind and body, the more you will feel love permeating your whole being.'

As my friend continued to practise the SSSSSH Technique, he found that through constant repetition he was able to feel this loving connection with Universal Consciousness more easily. If he were anxious or worried about something, he would stop, breathe, smile and connect with his heart. He found by doing this, and looking at whatever the issue was in his life, he was able to shift his perspective from his head to his heart. In doing so he experienced a sense of peace as he became calmer. As a result, he also gained a deeper mental clarity and, on many occasions, solutions appeared that he had not previously envisioned.

Within a couple of months, my friend increasingly felt strength, love, compassion and joy from within. This had been inconceivable to him before. He confided in me that he had spent many years looking outside of himself for answers and solutions to the stresses in his life.

He learned for the first time that all the answers lie within.

He realised that everything that he had searched for externally was already within. This was empowering for him. He saw that when he shifted his own energy from trying to change without to transforming from within, he no longer needed to try to manipulate or control the external circumstances in his life. Instead, by taking full responsibility for his own reaction to the various issues, he changed the whole trajectory of his life. Stresses from work to his personal life diminished, as new opportunities appeared which were closer to his soul's truth. He came to see that fear really was an illusion. This gave him greater courage to move forward in his life.

This did not happen overnight, but by the conscious moment-to-moment decision to choose love over fear. My friend did not have to experience a spiritual crisis to attain this heart connection and inspiration from his soul. All that was required was a willingness, on his part, to be open to the possibility of Divine Wisdom and faith to trust this guidance.

As he continued to practise this technique, he found that he became increasingly enthusiastic about life. Every time he chose to come from the love in his heart, as opposed to the fearful anxieties in his mind, he gained energy. This newfound energy was then available for living life in a more positive and joyful way, which encouraged him to keep going, as his life expanded in this new direction.

If you choose to try this SSSSSH Technique, it is so important to keep repeating, 'I feel love and radiate light,' not only when you are stressed but also during the quieter moments of life. Like depositing money in a savings account, if you continuously add more to the account, then as it increases you have a fund ready for that proverbial rainy day.

If you choose to repeat this exercise, you can shift the focus in your life from your head to your heart. You may at times find it easy, while on other occasions, it may be extremely challenging. It won't be a uniform trajectory. However, if you continue with the exercise, the general direction in which your energy moves will be a positive one. You may find that you gain greater mental clarity, access inspired insights and become more compassionate towards everyone. The more you practise, the more this becomes your daily reality. To quote John Irving's Owen Meany, 'Faith takes practice.'

The SSSSSH Technique is a simple but powerfully effective way to find your limiting thoughts and beliefs. Make the statement to yourself, 'I feel love and radiate light,' and then gently allow yourself to *listen* to the thoughts that come into your consciousness, *feel* your emotions and *sense* how your whole body feels. If you quietly observe, you may find that many thoughts appear and more than likely they are not conducive to creating your best life. If they are not aligned with creating the joy you wish for in your life, allow yourself to quietly observe these thoughts.

Instead of berating yourself for having these thoughts and emotions, congratulate yourself for having the courage to acknowledge them. Then gently choose to let these thoughts which are not constructive in your life go. Slowly but surely, you will find that you begin to feel more centred in your heart and connected with your soul with each choice of love over fear.

The key to making this work is to consciously shift your centre of attention from your head to your heart by keeping your focus on feeling and experiencing the pure love of your soul and Universal Consciousness. From this broader perspective, you liberate yourself to live your soul's truth of pure love. You become love when you allow the pure love of Universal Consciousness to flow through you and guide your life.

The more you feel love in your heart in the present moment, the more you look at all aspects of yourself through the loving eyes of your soul, as opposed to the critical eyes of your mind. Listen to the thoughts that float up to the surface of your consciousness, like debris washed upon the shore after a storm. By first accepting them and then moment to moment consciously deciding to let them go, you eventually find that this deep inner heart connection and peace become your normal state of being.

It is amazing how, as children, we soak up other people's ideas and thoughts so deeply that they become part of our own lives. Unconsciously, we all create core beliefs which manifest as consequential patterns. Whether misconstrued or misunderstood, by challenging them now we can choose to either keep them, if they have a positive influence in our lives, or if they do not help us, to let them go in the present moment.

Similarly, we often carry emotions from the past which prevent us from fully living and loving life now. When we live unconsciously we are often trapped by our thoughts, continuously repeating patterns of the past or projecting into the future; either way, we are not living now. Even if there are emotions or situations in your life that you think you cannot change, you can always change your perspective about them and create a sense of tranquillity. By continuously using the SSSSSH Technique to become more heart-centred, the energy that you bring to situations will no longer be negative and will at least be neutral, thus opening the possibility for divinely inspired solutions to appear.

Think about incorporating this technique throughout your day, in all aspects of your life, from the first few minutes of your day when you wake up, to waiting at traffic lights, when you are exercising, or standing in the queue at the supermarket. By continuously repeating, 'I feel love and radiate light,' whenever you can, you access this infinite wellspring of stillness within and automatically reconnect with the pure love of Universal Consciousness.

You may wish to say the words out loud when you are on your own, or quietly in your own mind when you are out and about in your daily life. If your hand is free, just gently touch your heart with the tips of your index and middle finger, as if you were adjusting a button on a shirt. The key is to find whatever works for you and to keep practising. In my friend's case, he began to use this technique every morning on his 20-minute underground train ride to work. By this choice, in addition to changing the drudgery of a daily commute to a more enjoyable experience, he has also transformed his entire day by allowing the love of his soul and Universal Consciousness guide him throughout his day.

You may even find that 'I feel love and radiate light,' keeps automatically repeating in your mind. As a consequence of the energy of these thoughts, you create the opportunity for your feelings and whole body to be light and vibrant. You may find yourself becoming kinder and more compassionate towards yourself and others, as you become a catalyst and conduit for the pure love of Universal Consciousness.

Through constant repetition you may find that you actually become one with this light, joyful state. Rather than it being the exception, it becomes your normal state of being.

As this becomes your norm, you know when something is out of kilter if for some reason you no longer feel centred in your heart. It feels unusual and strange. Stop. Become still. Breathe slowly. Smile. Yes, smile, and say, 'I feel love and radiate light,' as you gently touch your heart and give yourself credit for that moment of being centred in your heart because you truly are. Listen quietly to the non-constructive thoughts. By accepting and choosing to release them, you can regain your natural heart-centred joyful balance, moment to moment, as you reconnect with your soul. Like every new habit, it takes the decision to make this a priority in your life and then the persistence to keep practising it again, and again and again.

As you maintain your intention to *feel love*, you naturally align with the love of Universal Consciousness. As you receive this love, you automatically radiate this love, sharing it with everyone you touch in your life. At this higher vibration of love, because this is the energy frequency that you are emitting, you open the doorway for attracting more love back into your life.

Dare to imagine what your life would be like, moment to moment, experiencing the oneness of pure love of Universal Consciousness. Are you willing to allow yourself to feel love and radiate light to create your best life now?

There are only two ways to live your life. One is as though nothing is a miracle. The other is as if everything is.
    Albert Einstein

A true paradigm shift occurs for us, not externally in the outer world, but from within by realising that we co-create our 'reality'. By moving from our heads to our hearts, we reconnect with our deepest level of truth – the Source energy of love. We recognise that we are already whole. We are part of the eternal light of Universal Consciousness. By allowing the pure love of Universal Consciousness flow through us, we naturally feel a joy, enthusiasm and even exuberance for life and this is how we can create the life of our dreams. When we make the choice to come from love, our lives expand in ways far beyond the limited thinking of our restrictive minds.

PART 3

INSPIRATIONAL TECHNIQUES FOR LIVING AND LOVING YOUR LIFE

Let yourself be silently guided by the strength of pull of what you really love.
Rumi

One of the greatest gifts of my NDE is that I experience this beautiful energy every day. Of course there are times when I get completely distracted and totally 'lose the plot'. But by simply refocusing, knowing that everyone and everything are created from pure light and energy, life flows once again. I am aware of the energy that I bring to all situations and share with people, and I am also equally aware of the energy of the people that I meet on this journey through life. The energy that we emit affects not only our own lives, but also touches the lives of those close to us and ripples outwards. I believe that life is about coming from the heart, treating everyone with respect, sharing the light that is within us all, and giving back in whatever way we can.

By simply choosing to open up to the possibility of the existence of Universal Consciousness, you can become the co-creator of your own life. If you set the intention to feel love, or at least be open to the possibility, then you can change any situation which is not part of your truth. Even if you cannot alter the circumstances, you can still modify your thoughts, changing not only how you feel, but also your experience of the situation. No matter how insurmountable the problems in our everyday lives may appear, the solution is always at hand. If you consciously choose to align with the same energy that has created galaxies, oceans, mountains and continuously breathes life and energy into every living creature, you tap into the never-ending pool of potential which is available to create your best life. In doing so, you also allow this energy to work in the best interests of everyone you touch in your lifetime.

If you choose to live in a more heart-centred way, the practical tools and ideas below may assist you with receiving your own Divine guidance. You may have already learned some of these techniques, or many of them may be new to you; either way is perfect. What I intend to share is *why* they work based on my experience of the NDE and also give examples of *how* they work.

When you allow this infinite Source of power, potential and possibilities to work through you, you co-create your greatest life.

I) AFFIRMATIONS

We are not human beings having a spiritual experience. We are spiritual beings having a human experience.
     Pierre Teilhard de Chardin

We choose to take life's journey either consciously or unconsciously. If we decide to live consciously, we become aware that we are spiritual beings in physical bodies, creating our realities through the interaction with a Greater Power. Every time we consciously choose to live in the moment, with love from our hearts, we connect with this Divine Wisdom.

If, however, we choose to live unconsciously, it is often with fear-based thinking, blaming and criticising others and circumstances in our lives. We create power struggles and continue to lose this soul connection by making decisions from scarcity and fear. When we live unconsciously, we become limited by our perceptions, and frequently feel disconnected and disempowered.

Affirmations can provide a powerful way of aligning with our souls' truths. If you think that affirmations might be cliché or possibly too new-age for you, consider stopping for a few minutes and listen to the stream of unconscious thoughts playing in your mind. Are your thoughts positive? Are they constructive? Are they in line with the life you wish to lead? Or would you maybe benefit from consciously choosing some positive thoughts?

Anytime, anywhere, you can stop and reconnect with your heart. If you choose to live life in a more heart-centred manner, then you may wish to become still and allow yourself to delve within your heart to feel your deepest truth and soul's desire. What would you love to create with your life? What would be your highest potential and in the best interests of those you touch in your life?

Rather than focusing on a specific outcome of a certain thing that you would like, please would you consider the possibility of setting a more powerful intention from your soul? If you choose this, then you open yourself to unforeseen opportunities and blessings.

The key is to connect with your heart and soul – which you can do by using the SSSSSH Technique. From this centred place, you can choose an affirmation which expresses your deepest truth. You may like to say, 'I feel deep inner peace now,' if peace is what you yearn for in your life. Or, 'I feel joy now,' if you desire joy in your life. Whatever you wish to reconnect with and create more of in your life, this can be your affirmation.

A simple, powerful and extremely effective affirmation is 'I love life!' By feeling your love for life, you immediately become centred in your heart while your mind simultaneously becomes focused on living now, in this present moment. You become empowered by reconnecting with the pure love of Universal Consciousness, allowing your natural radiance to shine through. The more often you repeat this affirmation, the more you shift your energetic vibration to resonate at this higher frequency. As you attune your frequency to this higher vibration of love, the easier it becomes to manifest this love in your life.

Years ago, before my NDE, I chose to say, 'I am love, light, beauty and truth' as my daily affirmation. Now, many years later, I am sharing the experience of *love* from my NDE, as Artist of the *Light*, in an art form that is *beautiful*, for people to access their souls' *truths*.

Similarly, when I was in the ICU of the hospital, I was guided to 'surrender to the bliss'. I relaxed into this state, and allowed the Divine Wisdom of Universal Consciousness to heal me. After my NDE, I decided to fully integrate all of the blissful energy I had experienced, so I repeated these words again and again until I completely merged with the oneness. It is still a great affirmation to use if ever I find myself disconnected from the feeling of love and soulful peace.

What affirmation would you choose to create your best life? Are you willing to experiment to see how much you could improve your life now?

2) MEDITATION AND THE POWER OF PRAYER

> *There is a quiet light that shines in every heart. Though it is always secretly there, it draws no attention to itself. It is what illuminates our minds to see beauty, our desire to seek possibility and our hearts to love life ... This shy inner light is what enables us to recognise and receive our very presence here as a blessing.*
>
> John O'Donohue

Meditation provides another way of connecting with Universal Consciousness. Through the power of meditation, by being able to relax mentally and physically, we can open our hearts to feel more alive while experiencing an inner peace which enables us to receive our souls' guidance.

Upon waking in the morning, the first few minutes are often the easiest time of the day to make this heart and soul connection. This is because we are still partly in a dreamlike state. We are therefore more fluid in our thoughts and perspectives. It is also by far the most powerful time of day because we can clearly set the intention to be guided by this wisdom throughout the entire day. As a consequence, moments of spontaneous insight, inspired perceptions and ideas flow, directing the day in accordance with Divine Wisdom.

People often say that they do not have time to meditate or pray, or even be still, in their daily lives. This is understandable in our fast-paced modern society. However, the great irony is that when we are so busy and can't find the time to meditate, this is when we are most in need of inner stillness. By becoming more heart-centred, we can actually gain mental clarity and a greater vision for our lives, saving time inadvertently spent in ways which were not aligned with our truths.

If you don't have the time for a long meditation, even a few minutes are enough to allow your soul guide your thoughts. Meditating or praying can appear daunting at times: where do you begin? There are many wonderful ways to meditate and pray. What is most important is to find a way that resonates with you. The key is to start somewhere, anywhere. It really does not matter, just begin. Your mind could tie you up in knots as to which is the best method for meditating: should I use a mantra, should I stare at a candle, or contemplate a beautiful rose? There is no right way, there is only your way and that commences as soon as you make the decision to include meditation or prayer in your life.

If you wish to meditate, a simple way to begin is to open your heart, connect with your soul and let the stillness arise from within. You may choose to use the SSSSSH Technique to assist you with this. When you become centred, allow yourself to be guided and shown your true path.

For an example of the power of meditation and prayer, I wish to share the story of a friend of mine who was struggling to find peace in his life, and found what he was looking for in the most beautiful of ways.

As a Christian, my friend resonated with the Prayer of St Patrick, in particular the line, 'May Christ be in us'. To reinforce this meditative prayer, he tried searching for an inspiring image of Christ radiating light from his heart. One Sunday while at Mass, he looked up and saw that the stained glass image in the centre window high above the altar was exactly that image of Christ. It was a beautiful sunny morning, and the sun shone directly through that glass, radiating light from Christ's heart. He smiled when he realised that although he had attended that church for over 16 years, he had never noticed the image before. It had been there for all those years, but it was through shifting his attention to love and peace that his perception had changed, allowing him to have this experience.

Are you willing to open your heart and reconnect with the love of Universal Consciousness through the power of mediation or prayer?

3) RECEIVE DIVINE GUIDANCE IN YOUR LIFE

When we are no longer able to change a situation, we are challenged to change ourselves.
Viktor Frankl

If we are truly honest with ourselves, we see that we often make choices simply from habit. We have always done it a certain way, so why change? The momentum of energy creates a path in a particular direction. If this path is not created in alignment with the direction of our inner truths, then we can consciously choose to change the direction. Divine Wisdom is within and all around us, always encouraging us to find our highest path.

This Source of wisdom is constantly speaking to us. The question is: are we listening? We receive gentle whispers at first, and they become more frequent and louder if we still refuse to listen. It can seem that life is flowing beautifully; then suddenly we are hit by a tidal wave of some crisis of health, career or a huge financial loss. Although the situation may appear to be overwhelming, it may actually be Divine Wisdom's greatest gift. Even if we cannot understand why it is happening, by having the faith to trust that this is an opportunity for growth, we can open up to the possibility of a solution.

A friend and I were speaking recently about how we get these signs throughout life, if we choose to pay attention. He said that he always experiences gentle messages, showing him that he needs to make adjustments in his life. In other words, he makes the necessary changes before the situation becomes a serious illness or some other form of crisis. I, on the other hand, was deaf as a doorpost to providential signs, up until my mid-twenties. I had no belief in the existence of anything outside of the material realm. It was not part of my perspective on life. I had to be bed-bound, in a darkened room, barely able to move my eyes, before I began to listen. Later, through the experience of my NDE, I learned to hear and appreciate these messages.

Every time I make the choice to completely surrender to Universal Consciousness, the new-found depth and wisdom I find stays with me, like a buried treasure brought to light. I am given the gift of another part of my soul to guide and serve as I move forward in my life. No matter how tough times can appear to be, there are always opportunities to connect more deeply within and then share more love and light in this world.

It was devastating when I ended my marriage and lost both of my parents, all within a ten-week period at the end of 2010. One of my dearest friends commented that my life was making Shakespeare's *Hamlet* look like a comedy! How right he was. After having lost the three closest people whom I dearly loved, there was a gaping void in my life and I felt empty. I had the choice to either crawl under the bedcover and never come out again, or slowly learn to rebuild my life.

I realised that although I had no control over the choices of my ex-husband or deaths of my parents, I did have the freedom to choose how I would respond to these circumstances. I decided to trust and have a profound faith. I chose to centre in the stillness of my soul, be present and be willing to let go with love. Although on the human level this was extremely challenging, by embracing Divine Wisdom and choosing to see through the compassionate eyes of my soul, I was eventually able to regain my inner peace.

Life constantly changes. If we can follow an approach

of non-attachment, so that our sense of who we are does not depend on anything or anyone, i.e. a relationship, job, title, etc., we can choose to anchor firmly in our souls' truths and allow our lives to be directed by Universal Consciousness. The old adage 'Time heals all wounds' can really be true, especially if we choose to focus on living from our hearts.

Are you willing to allow yourself to receive the guidance of Divine Wisdom in your life?

4) VISION FOR YOUR LIFE

Walk with the dreamers, the believers, the courageous,
the cheerful, the planners, the doers, the successful
people with their heads in the clouds and their feet
on the ground.
   Wilfred Peterson

To create the vision for your life, find whatever feels like the best way for you to tap into your truth and connect with your soul. As I mentioned earlier, there are many ways of doing this. Some people connect through nature, being by the sea or in a forest. Others feel that sense of inner peace by listening to music, singing or laughing with friends. For a lot of people, meditation, yoga, running or dancing assist them to find harmony within. It does not matter how you connect; the key is to find the way, or ways in which you feel this inner peace and then make the decision to have this connection as a priority in your life.

Like any good habit, it is essential to make this part of your daily routine to fully receive the benefits. If you choose to do this, your energy and time can become more focused on the real priorities in your life. The superficial issues that once appeared so important may disappear, as a quiet serenity permeates your life.

Synchronicities occur as Divine Wisdom provides signals showing that you are on track. Life then unfolds in ways that you could never have conceived of before. This continues again and again until you reach the point where you wonder how you ever lived your life without this being part of your daily existence.

The more you create the vision to live from the essence of your soul, the more your soul's beauty can shine through, bringing positive change not only in your own life but also in the lives of all those around you. As you become increasingly inspired, you create the opportunity for others to also access their inner truths and purpose in life. As this expands, your ignited soul becomes the catalyst for more souls to embrace their light.

I was fortunate to meet an Irish couple in the US who have a passion for life and vision for being of service to humanity that is so compelling, it becomes infectious. I met Dr Pearse Lyons and his wife, Deirdre, through providence, at the Ireland – US Council's 50th anniversary dinner in New York. They made such a positive impression on me that I have not been the same person since meeting them.

Dr Lyons was the honouree at the dinner. He gave a wonderfully inspiring speech, clearly communicating from his heart. He spoke of the five Ds – Dream, Dare, Desire, Dedicate and Determination – and how, by following his sense of curiosity, he has created the vision for his company. One of their current research projects is developing a drug to treat Alzheimer's disease. Dr Lyons gave such a rousing speech that I was fascinated and wanted to learn more. My mother had suffered from a similar illness and with the thought of such an incredible drug becoming a reality, I knew I had to take the opportunity to speak with him. I waited until after the dinner and then introduced myself. We had a wonderful conversation.

I learned that, in addition to their research on Alzheimer's, his company is dedicated to trying to help resolve the world's expanding food needs associated with the burgeoning global population which is predicted to reach over nine billion people by 2050. Through their cutting-edge technology in the field of genetics, they are revolutionising food production worldwide by doubling crop productivity using natural methods. By placing the emphasis on long-term sustainability in pragmatic ways, they are changing all sectors of agriculture.

Their objective is also to change the industry norm away from manufacturing synthetic fertilisers, towards the production of fertilisers derived from natural sources. By improving the quality of food produced globally, this could have a huge impact on people's health worldwide.

They redefine the word 'visionary' in their dedication to creating a better quality of life on this planet. The business has been so successful because of its integrity. It is in the DNA of the company. It is the core principle, upon which everything is based, from the products to the consumers, from research to the environment, from education to philanthropy. Their vision encourages me every day to create an even bigger vision for my life. I am grateful for their inspiration.

By tapping into your soul, and opening up to the possibility of a Divine Consciousness, you can find your own vision for creating the life you are meant to live and how you can be of service.

What is the vision you are creating for your life?

5) SET INTENTIONS

Everything exposed by the light becomes visible —
and everything that is illuminated becomes a light.
St Paul, Ephesians 5:14

If we choose to align our intentions with our souls' truths, in addition to tapping into the powerful Source of Universal Consciousness, the momentum of this energy becomes channelled in a positive direction.

On a crisp New Year's Eve, a friend and I decided to take a walk along the Mall in Washington, D.C. to celebrate the coming of the New Year. Rather than making New Year's resolutions, I like to reflect on the year gone by and then focus my energy on setting the highest intentions for the coming year. That night, I chose to reset the intention to come from the light and share this from my heart.

As we approached the Lincoln Memorial, to our amazement, we saw thousands of small candles illuminating the entire perimeter of the Reflecting Pool. The candles were glowing and flickering in the darkness. This was the first time that the Reflecting Pool had been lit up in this manner. It was a special occasion commemorating the 150th anniversary of the Emancipation Proclamation, granting slaves their freedom.

As I sat quietly contemplating the light, staring at the myriad of candles shining like beacons of hope in the darkness, I realised that true freedom is not just a physical state but a mental and emotional one. Liberty is found in a peaceful heart and still mind. It is freedom from the enslavement of constant noise, distraction and negative thoughts of the mind. From this place of light within, the shadows and darkness of ego disappear as the soul shines brightly. By setting the intention to come from our hearts throughout the day, we create the possibility for our minds to quieten. We cannot be in fear and in love at the same moment in time, so the obsessive, relentless chatter in our minds slows down when we live from our hearts with love.

Initially though, when we focus on the silence and stillness, many thoughts and fears come up to be released. If we can be clear in our intention of coming from our hearts, while aligning with our souls, then there is no need to renounce the shadow or banish the ego. Instead, by facing these fears and embracing our souls, love naturally appears and increases exponentially with each moment's choice of love over fear.

The Reflecting Pool had mirrored back to me an illuminated path and direction for the New Year. This was reinforced when I opened my calendar on New Year's Day. The image for January was of a beautiful Celtic cauldron with the words 'May we receive the light now.' The New Year began with a clear and focused intention of receiving my soul's Divine Light and sharing this love from my heart.

By setting clear intentions, you can align with the power of Universal Consciousness and allow it to co-create your life. Intentions can be thoughts in your mind, spoken verbally, written in your journal or made visual by the use of vision boards. The key is to find what works best for you, and then to come from your heart and create this in your life.

What are your intentions for creating your best life?

6) JOY AND FOLLOW YOUR PASSION

> *A cheerful heart is good medicine.*
> Proverbs 17:22

Joy can be our natural state, if we choose love, regardless of what is occurring in our day-to-day lives. Many traditional cultures have recognised this truth throughout the centuries. This is the energy which creates opportunities, because all the fear-based barriers simply dissolve into the ethers, as the light-filled energy continues in this positive direction. By simply asking: *what brings me the greatest joy, right here and right now?* we open up to receiving more joy in our lives. Through following our passions and surrounding ourselves with people who love, support and encourage us, we naturally become aligned with our souls' truths and can share our gifts with others.

One person who inspires me greatly is Sir James Galway. As a young girl growing up in Ireland, it was always a treat to hear him playing his flute on the television. Whenever he appeared on the screen, our home came to a standstill as we all listened to his beautiful music.

Years later, I met Sir James on a few occasions and he always struck me as one of the most joyful people I have ever known. He has a passion for music and shares this with everyone, from audiences around the world, to teaching young aspiring flautists. From the first note he plays, he captures the audience's hearts. I said this to him after one of his performances. He beamed back with a mischievous grin on his face and said in his strong Belfast accent, 'Róisín, sure we close the doors after they enter the auditorium, so they can't escape!' Nobody would wish to, as it is a joy and a sheer delight to be in his company and experience his musical talents.

Róisín Fitzpatrick

They say that the best things in life are free. Well, I think a donation of a few dollars comes pretty close, what do you think? As the sweltering heat of a typical New York summer's day subsides at around 6 p.m., people of all ages from all walks of life and cultural backgrounds congregate at Shakespeare's statue in Central Park. They arrive there every Saturday evening, wearing casual jeans but with sequinned shoes adorning their feet. Everyone is drawn together by one passion – tango!

After the talcum powder is shaken over the stone pavement, transforming a hard stone surface into an outdoor dance floor, the Latin music commences. Then the worn black felt hat is passed around, where if you wish, you can throw in a few dollars to dance the evening away.

My friend Denise and I used to meet there regularly during the summer months, jokingly jostling each other, vying for one elderly gentleman in particular who was able to glide his lucky dance partner with exquisite elegance over the polished paving. Even if I clumsily trod on this poor gentleman's toes, with wonderful etiquette, he would simply smile and say, 'Oh, don't worry, that did not hurt at all,' though I am sure he felt like amputating his toe with the pain! It was a joy to dance with everyone, amateurs and aficionados alike. It was equally mesmerising to see all the couples dancing in unison under Shakespeare's watchful eye. Do you know of a more joyful way to spend a few dollars in central Manhattan?

Are you open to giving and receiving joy in your life?

7) FORGIVENESS AND COMPASSION

Without forgiveness, there's no future.
Archbishop Desmond Tutu

Many years ago, I remember reading books on the subject of forgiveness. Although I vaguely understood the general concept, I became quite baffled when forgiveness was spoken of as being one of the most loving things that we could do for ourselves. However, after my NDE, this all made perfect sense because I realised that I am, as everyone is, pure energy. If we can take 100% responsibility for our energy and our emotions, we can create our best lives through sharing our light in this world.

If we recognise that we are light-filled energy beings, then when we are emotionally clear, this love and light can flow in an unobstructed manner. If, however, we are 'holding on to grudges', then we are quite literally hoarding the negative emotions. These emotions are like discolorations or blotches on this light energy. By firstly acknowledging, then truly experiencing them with the intention of surrendering and letting them go, or releasing them to a Divine Power, we can become freer, lighter and more energised. Instead of emitting a dimmed, obscure, darkened vibration out into the world, we can radically shift this to share our souls' loving energy. This is the frequency we then experience in our daily lives.

To proactively choose to connect with love in our hearts is a decision, rather than reactively coming from fear and projecting negative emotions and energy. When we share our souls' light, this is the deepest truth of who we really are. The more regularly we choose this, the more we serve our own best interest and the interests of those whom we meet throughout life. Forgiveness is truly one of the greatest gifts that we can give to ourselves and others.

Forgiveness is not a superficial saying of 'I let this go' while ardently stewing in the negative emotions or pretentiously taking the moral high ground. I had a laugh with one of my friends recently when he made a mistake over a small issue. It really was not important but I joked with him, 'Oh, you are in big trouble for that one. That's a mortler!' (colloquial way of saying a mortal sin), all the while laughing to myself. Lo and behold, within five minutes I then realised that I had made a huge mistake a few minutes earlier, which my friend had already seen but graciously forgiven. I was totally embarrassed and apologised immediately.

He said, 'I forgave you.' This was all perfect if he had left it at that, but alas, he continued audaciously saying, 'I took the high ground, Róisín.' As soon as those words left his lips, he began laughing at himself. 'I just fell off that moral high ground, didn't I?'

'Yes, you did,' I smiled, 'and it was a spectacular crash-landing off that precipice!'

So we were quits after all.

Forgiveness has no moral high ground. Everyone is equal and recognised as such. It really is about totally *releasing all judgement* about yourself and everyone else. This does not mean being less than who we are, so another person can feel more than who they are. Quite the opposite, it means respecting everyone as being equal. It requires taking full responsibility for our own emotions and quietly, but resolutely, staying fully connected with our souls' light and sharing our own unique beauty in this world.

Forgiveness can often be perceived as a weakness, as if it condones or excuses behaviour which is unacceptable, lets people 'off the hook', or 'allows them to win'. The great irony is that the person holding on to these negative thoughts and emotions is the only person guaranteed to feel all of them.

Forgiveness is never a weakness; it is one of our greatest strengths.

We are all energy beings, and we choose, consciously or unconsciously, the frequency at which we vibrate. If we hold onto any negative emotions by blaming others, self-pitying, or feeling resentment or injustice, then we are the ones who are kept on the 'hook' which we have created in our own minds. We don't 'win' anything, but only lose the precious time that we have to live life – a life filled with love. Letting another person 'off the hook' automatically releases us to become lighter, empowered and stronger. So why on earth would we choose this, when the alternatives are lightness, freedom, joy and peace? Quite simply, because we are all human, replete with all our human frailties.

If we choose not to 'let them off the hook' and stubbornly hang on to every morsel of hatred, bitterness, anger just to be sure that they don't 'get away with it', who are we cheating in life? Nobody but ourselves. We are the ones making the choices.

If somebody has treated you in an unloving manner, they dim their own light, deny themselves the freedom and joy that come from a clear soul connection, and block themselves from experiencing their soul's love. As long as they continue to behave in this way, they deceive themselves at a much deeper level because this is the energy vibration they experience and feel in daily life.

Irrespective of other people's choices for their lives, through forgiveness we can free ourselves, right here, right now, to live our best lives. Forgiveness is a choice that we can make, without the expectation of a response or acknowledgement from another person. It is within our own power to quietly release and bless everyone involved, including ourselves.

By making the choice to forgive and let go of the past, we free ourselves to create our best future. We all have access to the infinite Source of energy. When we become aligned with our souls' Divine Light, we create the opportunity for everyone we meet in our lifetime to connect with their soul's light. *The most loving action that we can take is full responsibility for the clarity of our own connection with Universal Consciousness and how we share this light in the world.*

If we can stand back from situations, be still and connect with Universal Consciousness, it becomes clear that negative emotions lower our frequency, block our flow of light and dampen our spirits. When we can let them go, which means not just superficially but really going into the depths of the emotions in order to release them, then we can fully reconnect with our souls' truths.

As a result we can experience a physical lightness, greater energy and vitality, emotional peace, mental clarity and spiritual freedom. So forgiving is really one of the greatest gifts that we can give to ourselves. Love is 'for-giving', to ourselves and to all those we meet, irrespective of the circumstances. To truly forgive takes time, and it makes no mistakes. In our full humanity, it will not always be an even, upward trajectory. Whether the negative thoughts and emotions are about you, or another person or people, or particular circumstances, it really does not matter. By allowing Divine Grace to enter into your life and cleanse any negative residual thoughts, those shadows become obliterated by the light. By being gentle with yourself and congratulating yourself for having the courage to face emotions, instead of being critical and berating yourself for having these negative feelings, or blaming others for them, the channel for Divine intervention opens. To go through the depths of these emotions, but all the while keeping a steady focus on the intention of forgiving, releasing and clearing, this strengthens your connection with the light.

Whether the issues are from your childhood, your current life or worries about the future, by continuously choosing to focus your attention on connecting with the loving light of your soul, in this present moment, you become love and free yourself and everyone involved. The eternal light of Universal Consciousness always shines. The question is: *are you allowing it to shine brightly through you?*

When we take full responsibility for everything in our lives that we have created, consciously or unconsciously, then challenges in life become opportunities. Even if we do not fully understand why certain events happen in our lives, or why we are experiencing certain emotions, if we can keep the faith and learn to forgive, then we can trust that they are opportunities to establish a stronger, more empowered and light-filled soul connection. It truly is a gift to develop the ability to see life this way.

If we can view this world and challenges through our souls' loving eyes, in addition to learning to forgive, we can also begin to feel compassion. Compassion is not something that needs to be attained or achieved, it flows naturally after we let go of all resistance and negative emotions.

Richard Moore, a native of Derry in Northern Ireland, was blinded by a rubber bullet when he was caught in crossfire on his way home from school during 'the Troubles'. He was only ten years of age on that fateful day. Although many people would have become embittered, resentful or angry, Richard managed through the power of forgiveness to create peace in his own mind, and he continued on to live a full life. When he became an adult, he married and had two daughters, ran a successful business and became a semi-professional musician. In 1996, he founded the charity Children in Crossfire, to focus on issues relating to children's health and education in developing countries.

Throughout these years he searched to find the British soldier who had shot him. In 2006, he met Charles and forgave him for his actions over 30 years earlier. Charles recognised that Richard was an innocent victim. This acknowledgement was important to Richard, who in turn, recognised that Charles regretted his actions when he later received these words in a letter from Charles; 'The shock has obviously gone, but the sadness and regret, though somewhat faded with the passage of time, are still there. And with the advantage of hindsight I wish I had not taken the action I did.' Both men have now moved on from their initial meeting and, against the odds, they have developed a genuine friendship based on forgiveness. They now collaborate together on many projects to bring hope into the lives of children around the world.

Are you taking full responsibility for the light you share in this world? Are you forgiving yourself and others so that you can radiate your full magnificence?

8) SYNCHRONICITIES

Whatever you can do, or dream you can do, begin it.
Boldness has a genius, power and magic in it.
   Goethe

When we align ourselves through love with Universal

Consciousness, we become part of the oneness of infinite possibilities and potential. As a result, we receive more synchronistic signs and serendipities. Divine Wisdom is always trying to guide us. The question is: *are we allowing ourselves to receive the messages?*

Recently, when I was flying from Sydney, Australia to Singapore, on a trip with my art, I met a flight attendant on the plane who came from Ireland. While speaking with her, I learned that she had also grown up in the same village, Howth, on the outskirts of Dublin. As we spoke, I realised to my amazement that her sister was the receptionist for our family doctor. When my parents were ill, her sister had been exceptionally kind to them. She had helped in so many ways when my family had needed urgent assistance with arranging prescriptions, liaising with the hospital for Dad or the nursing home for Mum.

It always astounds me how Divine Wisdom continuously provides signs and messages, in ways which are unforeseen or even unimaginable. There I was, on the other side of the globe from my home, 35,000 feet up in the air, and this connection was made. It was lovely to be able to let her know how grateful I was for her sister's kindness. I also felt that this was Mum and Dad guiding me on my life's journey. In a bittersweet moment, although it brought back all the emotional pain of losing my parents, it was a huge gift to be reminded that we are always guided by Divine Consciousness.

❂ ❂ ❂

When this book was almost finished and ready for submission to my editor, I remembered how the stained glass in my Granny Fitzpatrick's home had first awakened me to the beautiful synergy between glass and light, and how this was a catalyst for my later life. I wrote the passage describing my early childhood experience and then closed my computer, thinking that it was the last piece which brought the whole book together.

Later that morning, I happened to drive out to Howth and when I passed my granny's former home, I caught a quick glimpse of a huge bulldozer with a giant claw tearing what once was the family home apart. I immediately stopped the car, ran in with tears in my eyes as I looked at the empty space where most of the rear of the house had already been demolished. However, the front entranceway still stood intact.

I explained to the foreman that this had been my father's home and asked him if he could take a photo for me of the front door with the pillars before they were torn down. After he took the photo, within seconds the pillars came crashing to the ground.

Then I saw the stained glass, not the huge piece which was on the return of the stairway (that had been removed many years earlier), but the stained glass which surrounded the front door. It stood there in isolation; miraculously it had not been smashed to pieces. I quickly blurted out, 'Could I ever ask a huge favour? You won't believe this but I wrote about the stained glass in this house just this morning. Is there any way we could salvage that glass?' as I pointed to the arch of stained glass standing erect while surrounded by the heap of concrete and timber debris.

Martin was the foreman's name, and he was unbelievably kind to this blubbering stranger who was impinging on his day's work. 'Of course, wait here because it would be dangerous for you to be any closer.' He scrambled over the heap of shards and rubble and spoke with the operator of the bulldozer, who used the gigantic metal gripper to pull the frame from the foundations and swung it over, placing it carefully on the level ground. We then managed to save four of the panels of glass.

These stained glass panels are in my home now, creating a full circle from my early childhood to the present moment. My spirits become lifted every time I see the sunlight radiating through the coloured glass.

Are you allowing yourself to receive Divine inspiration throughout your life? Are you open to seeing the coincidences in your life and how empowering they can be in providing guidance for living your best life?

9) FAITH

Scepticism is the beginning of faith.
Oscar Wilde

Most of the time, I am blessed to be able to feel the blissful energy of the NDE by choosing to focus on coming from my heart. This is a gift to be able to feel the pure love of Universal Consciousness. Nonetheless, I am still here in a physical body with human fears and all that entails in day-to-day life. Whenever I find myself wrapped up in details and completely missing the point, I know that I have the choice to pull myself back again and centre in my soul. As a consequence, my life invariably takes off in a new and unforeseen way that leaves me bewildered as to why I ever doubted in the first place.

Recently, I was invited to a small dinner party in Washington, D.C. by my friend Susan Davis. She arranged a dinner with some of her close friends, including the then Irish Ambassador to the United States, H.E. Michael Collins, and his wife, Marie, as an opportunity for me to meet all of these people in an informal gathering.

I invited another friend, with whom I was staying, to join us for the dinner. After a few minutes at the dining table, Susan tapped her glass and announced, 'Now, everyone, please fill up your glasses. Róisín is going to tell us her story and all about the inspiration for her artworks.'

I had not expected this at all and I was totally unprepared. I had been creating art in Ireland for the summer and had not done any public speaking for over six months. Fortunately, the conversation was diverted for a few minutes, giving me enough time to gather my thoughts and then I began to talk. I was not sure how deeply I should speak about the spiritual component of my art, as I had never met most of the guests before, with the exception of Ambassador and Mrs Collins and my friend with whom I was staying. Susan reassured me, 'We are all friends here and we would love to hear your full story, Róisín.'

After describing my NDE as the source of inspiration for my artworks, I was asked many great questions as we discussed the real meaning of life and death. With the deeper questions, I was given the opportunity to share the details of the exquisite beauty of the light I experienced during the NDE.

I was grateful to Susan and also to everyone at the dinner party for their willingness to be open-minded. Susan's mother, who is in her mid-nineties, kept smiling at me throughout the evening. She explained that this is how she has lived her life so far, living every day from her heart. She is hugely compassionate, sharp as a tack, fully embraces life, and even works out with her personal trainer twice a week!

After the dinner, which had been wonderful, when I was back in my friend's house, I suddenly became emotionally upset. I could not stop crying. Initially, I was not aware why I was so distraught. I thought back to the dinner and remembered that I was asked, on numerous occasions during the evening, why I had chosen to return to this world after I had accessed such incredible bliss. Why would I ever come back here? I shared that the answer was because my parents were alive at the time and there was no way that I could leave them, as I knew it would be too painful for them. Then I realised why I was so upset. It was yet another challenge and a blessing.

I missed, and still miss, the profound feeling of love which is constant when in the non-physical realm. Naturally, I missed being in the infinite, unconditionally loving state. I can still access this at any moment I wish while here in the physical realm, but sometimes I have to make this choice, whereas in the other realm, it just is. Love is all that exists. Love is everywhere. Love is all-encompassing.

The original reason why I came back was for my parents, but as Mum and Dad had since passed over, that reason no longer existed. Though I am delighted for my parents, knowing that they are in a beautiful place, it was challenging to be left behind here on the earthly plane.

My friend was wonderful and stayed up with me into the small hours of the morning, as I sobbed uncontrollably on the couch. If only all the people at the dinner party could have seen me crying my eyes out – I felt like a hypocrite speaking about bliss and there I was in an emotional heap on the sofa. My friend threw his head back and laughed at the mere suggestion of this. He reminded me that of course it was normal to feel this way. Like everyone, I can at times let fear take over. I realised quickly that I needed to get over this fear and focus with clarity on coming from the light.

I reaffirmed my decision, there and then, to be fully present while I am still here in a physical body. It takes awareness and a choice to overcome the human fears, but when we make that decision with faith, we create the opportunity for amazing things to occur.

The following week, I travelled to Chicago and I experienced serendipity after serendipity. I felt like I was skating on ice as I glided through every day. It was my first visit to Chicago, and doors opened everywhere for my art. A friend of mine from Ireland had since moved there and she introduced me to members of the Irish-American community. Also, another woman arranged for me to speak at the Chicago Arts Club. I actually knew so many people in the audience that it was a sheer delight to see these friendly faces as I shared my art. Everyone I met throughout the week was kind and helpful. I also went to Boston and, once again, felt so connected and blessed with all that happened effortlessly. Even when I flew back to Ronald Reagan Airport in Washington D.C., I bumped into an old classmate with whom I had studied in Geneva years earlier, who drove me back to my friend's home.

I told my friend all the providential experiences that had happened during the week. He smiled and said, 'Well, you asked for this.'

I looked at him, perplexed by his comment.

'Róisín, you asked why you are here, and you were given your answer. You are sharing the light and, because of your faith, you are being assisted in every way to make this happen.'

Are you open to the possibility of the existence of a Higher Realm of consciousness? Are you willing to have faith in this Divine Wisdom?

10) FULL RESPONSIBILITY FOR SHARING YOUR LIGHT IN THIS WORLD

I realised that they had already taken everything from me except my mind and my heart. Those they could not take without my permission. I decided not to give them away.

Nelson Mandela

As humans, we often find it challenging to let go of negative emotions. If someone has treated us, or someone dear to us, in an unfair manner and caused either physical or emotional pain, our first reaction is often one of wanting to 'get even', to settle the score. What if, instead of taking it upon ourselves to be the judge and jury, we choose to surrender to a Higher Source of wisdom and seek a more inspired response?

I recently heard of a man who also had a life-altering NDE. When he went through his life review, he experienced all the pain that he had inflicted on others throughout his lifetime. Instead of coming from his own self-centred perspective, he took the place of the recipient and *he* suffered all the visceral pain.

When he was in his early twenties, during a fit of road rage, he had pummelled an innocent motorcyclist to a bloody pulp and abandoned him on the roadside. Now, in this life review, he had to endure the physical pain of each blow, again and again, but this time as the recipient of the lashed-out anger. This was not a form of punishment or judgement imposed on him by an angry God, but simply a rebalancing of energy at a higher level of consciousness. From this experience he learned a broader understanding of both this world and the world beyond.

Similarly, he experienced how when he was a small child he had picked some flowers from his grandmother's garden to give to her as a gift. However, he felt this from his grandmother's perspective, which was one of mixed joy and sadness. The happiness of receiving a gift from her grandson but sorrow that her treasured flowerbeds were ruined.

Examples like this show us how, when we can overcome our need to judge others and trust in the greater Divine plan, we free ourselves to live life without seeking any form of retaliation. The rebalancing of energy appears to be an integral part of a much grander perspective than we could ever master with our limited perception of life. This does not mean allowing others to take advantage. It simply means always respecting ourselves and others, and consciously choosing to focus on our higher purpose and meaning in life.

We have all done things that we regret. We look back and cringe as we see our actions and their impact on other people, wishing we could somehow rectify the situations. Thankfully, we can make things right again, here and now. Either in person, if the person is still alive and can be contacted, or in spirit, by truly surrendering to the Divine Source. This Divine Power is all-loving, fully compassionate, infinitely understanding and always willing to guide us in the direction of our highest potential. All it takes is our willingness to accept full responsibility for our actions and when we know better, we make more positive choices.

Are you taking full responsibility for your actions and trusting a Higher Source of wisdom?

11) CONNECT WITH UNIVERSAL CONSCIOUSNESS

You and I exist only because God is forever blowing his breath into our being.
Archbishop Desmond Tutu

An effective way of connecting with Universal Consciousness is to simply stop, look up at the stars and see ourselves as part of the vast expanse of the universe. By doing this, we can gain a clearer perspective on all aspects of our lives.

Whenever I am feeling trapped in a thought or limited in my thinking, I go out into nature and look at the stars. If there is no light pollution, it may even be possible to discern the starlit path of the Milky Way. I often think about our ancestors, who built the astronomically aligned megalithic monuments, such as Newgrange. They were not continuously distracted by the ephemeral output of mobile phones, the internet and modern media. The stars and the universe were their playground and source of inspiration.

We have a resource of deep wisdom available to us, all the time, if we choose to connect. When we consciously choose to trust and allow this Divine Wisdom to guide our perceptions, rather than staying on the merry-go-round of restricted thoughts, we can open up to this boundless source of knowledge and allow ourselves to be guided.

Are you willing to allow the infinite power of Universal Consciousness which creates all of life, the galaxies and the stars co-create this life with you?

12) VISUALISATION

May you recognise in your life the presence, power and light of your soul.
   May you realise that you are never alone, that your soul in its brightness and belonging connects you intimately with the rhythm of the universe.
   John O'Donohue

Another wonderful way of tapping into Universal Consciousness is through the technique of visualisation. This is well established as a powerful tool for making positive life changes. Even the simplest of imagery can be extremely effective. During my NDE, I learned that we are not solid in physical form, instead we are created from light-filled energy. When we tap into this Source of energy, by first visualising in our minds and then feeling the pure love of this energy in our hearts, we can consciously bring more of this energy into our lives.

Through doing simple visualisations, while smiling and breathing deeply, we naturally share the love from our hearts as we deepen our connection with Universal Consciousness. By recognising that the eternal light is the Divine Source from which we all originate, we can re-imagine ourselves with a whole new way of being, knowing and experiencing this world.

If we wish, we can consciously choose to share the eternal light with everyone we meet and everywhere we go, by seeing this light flowing in and around all situations and people. This creates the opportunity for everyone we encounter on life's journey to tap into their own inner light and the pure love of Universal Consciousness.

Another way to consciously tap into the infinity of the universe is to regularly envision the light of the star-filled universe streaming through your body. Feel this expansive loving energy flowing in through your heart and spreading throughout your entire being. Then visualise a beautiful cascade of crystalline light radiating out from your heart to infinity, as you become one with this powerful Source of energy. The more you practise this visualisation, the more effective it becomes as you shift to a much larger perception of life. By repeating the words 'I feel love and radiate light,' you amplify the power of this visualisation.

If we recognise that we are energy beings, then we can become more conscious of the energy that we share in this world. As our energy changes, it affects change in the world around us. Even if we are not in the physical presence of another person, by simply thinking of them with loving thoughts, we can send them light.

How many times have you thought of someone, then unexpectedly received a call from them or accidentally bumped into them? How many stories have we heard of the healing power of prayer? If we recognise that we are always emitting energy the question is: *what are we sharing with this world? Are we sharing a light-filled, loving vibrational energy to enhance the lives of others?*

As a child growing up we did not have any pets in our family, so I was not used to animals. As a matter of fact, I was actually quite afraid of them, especially dogs because I was attacked by one when I was six years old. So, by choice, I would have always given animals, especially of the canine variety, a wide berth. However, since my NDE, I have repeatedly noticed a strange occurrence whenever I happen to be in the company of animals. They tend to approach me and become very calm. I honestly find this to be quite bizarre. But this keeps happening, over and over again, so it is more than a coincidence.

When I was staying in Washington D.C. on the night of the US presidential elections, I drove with a friend of mine, Dan, to the house of one of my friends from my days in Geneva. When we arrived, his dog was jumping all over the place and spinning around in circles, chasing his tail nervously. My friend said to us, 'Don't worry, he is a bit skittish but he won't harm you. It takes him

years to relax with people he does not know.' Dan loves
dogs, so he was trying to get his attention but the dog
was having none of this. The only time the dog looked at
Dan was to size up his ankle as an appetiser for dinner!

Yet within a few minutes, the dog came over to me.
To everyone's amazement, he sat quietly on the floor. He
gently rested his furry body against my winter boots.
Then after another few minutes, he jumped up beside me
on the couch. To everyone's astonishment, he nuzzled
his way onto my lap, like a sleeping child. If I moved to
go anywhere, he followed me. Dan kept saying to the
dog, 'Have some dignity, please!' and we all laughed.

As I visited different friends' homes in D.C. this kept
happening, over and over again. Dogs and cats would
come to me and quietly sit by my side or on my lap,
sticking to me like Velcro. Dan jokingly nicknamed me
Dr Doolittle. This light-hearted example shows how we
are energy – of the canine and non-canine variety – and
we share our energy in this world.

*What energy are you choosing to share? Are you sharing
your natural radiance with others?*

13) OPEN TO POSSIBILITIES

> *As soon as you trust yourself, you will know how to
> live.*
>
> Goethe

If we become open to receiving messages from Divine
Wisdom, we can experience an infinite number of
opportunities and possibilities in all areas of our lives.

There is no 'one way', but instead a myriad of different ways for us to align with our true selves. Divine Wisdom is always gently guiding us to take our highest path. If we choose not to take one route, another will present itself, and another, and another, and so on and so forth.

When we are in a state of joy, we automatically become aligned with our souls' truths. This is when we are at our most creative, most productive and can manifest effortlessly in the physical dimension of the material world. When we are filled with enthusiasm, we tap into the infinite Source of Universal Consciousness. We know we are connected when we feel a natural exuberance, lose all sense of time and wish to share this zest for life with everyone. As we open up to the boundless possibilities, life unfolds before us in wondrous ways.

An example of this occurred on one occasion when I went to Washington, D.C. for a weekend. On the Friday evening when I arrived, I went to the Jefferson Memorial with a friend of mine. It was a gorgeous summer's evening. As we sat on the steps leading up to the memorial, I told him that I had just experienced an amazing couple of weeks, as many serendipities were happening regarding the art and people were being incredibly supportive. During the same few weeks, he had experienced a challenging time at work. He stared at me inquisitively and asked, 'How do you do this?'

I replied, 'I simply choose to come from joy and align with Divine guidance, and then naturally find myself in the right place, at the right time. By letting go, I let Divine Grace direct my life.'

With that, a young man came over and asked us to take a photograph with his girlfriend. We were delighted to help and talked with them for a few minutes. They thanked us and walked towards the water's edge. My friend and I went back to sit on the steps once again.

A few minutes later, the same couple came rushing back to us, with a whole group of people shouting and laughing. We had no clue what was happening. Then they told us that they had just become engaged to be married. He had kept the ring concealed in his sock the whole time that they were nattering with us. She was not aware of it at the time, but their families had been hiding behind the pillars of the memorial waiting for the proposal.

They kindly invited us to join them in their celebration. The newly engaged couple were smiling joyfully as champagne flowed, cameras clicked and everyone was filled with love and happiness. My friend just kept staring at me with wide-open eyes. Then he said quietly and with a smile, 'OK, I get it, this really does work.'

This is an example of the bounteous joy waiting for us when we move beyond limited thinking and open up to the possibilities of Universal Consciousness. Life can unfold in wondrous ways.

Are you open to the boundless possibilities of Universal Consciousness?

14) SILENT RETREAT

*There are many ways of going forward, but only one
way of standing still.*
   Franklin D. Roosevelt

Since the NDE, my whole perspective of life and living
has broadened. I understand the importance of creating a
space for silence. It is difficult to hear our souls' guidance
over the turbulence of the mind. Being in silence is one of
the greatest techniques for accessing our inner wisdom.

   You may wish to use the SSSSSH Technique to assist
you with tapping into this silence within. These results
can be magnified by deliberately choosing to go to a
place of silent retreat, for a few minutes, hours, or days,
depending on the time you can make available. You
could create this space by taking a walk in nature, or
sitting comfortably in your favourite chair, relaxing by
a warm fire, or watching a star-filled sky, whatever feels
right for you. For the time that you set aside to be in
this place of silence, it is important to remove yourself
from all distractions such as mobile phones, television
or radio.

   Initially, you may be more aware of all the noise and
chatter of the mind and this can be frustrating. However,
if you make the choice, *moment by moment*, to stay in
your heart and focus on being in the silence, eventually
the overriding peace of your soul will envelop you and
encourage you to keep on this path.

When you come out of your silent retreat, all that you have accessed can be available to you at anytime, anywhere, by choosing to feel and experience this inner peace once again. If you decide to make inner peace a priority in your life, by continuously choosing peace over chaos, harmony over distractions, tranquillity over turmoil, many of the non-constructive thoughts naturally disappear. As you become more centred and connected, you may become clearer in your thinking and feel increasing joy in your heart.

When you return from this silence, and before engaging in communication, try to stay centred in this point of stillness. Ask yourself if your words improve upon the silence. Are you contributing anything of value? Are you sharing from your soul in an authentic way? Does the other person feel better after speaking with you? Is there kindness and compassion in your vocabulary, tone, body language and overall communication?

Are you willing to give yourself the gift of silence to access your soul's wisdom, positively impacting your own life and the lives of others?

15) GRATITUDE FOR LIFE, HEALTH, FAMILY AND FRIENDS

Wake at dawn with a winged heart and give thanks
for another day of loving.
    Kahlil Gibran

When I had the NDE, I realised that our true essence is pure energy. I merged with a dynamic Source which was brimming with creative potential. This energy overflows with possibilities. When we choose to focus our thoughts on love and gratitude, we then feel love and gratitude. Once we allow ourselves to feel love and gratitude, we then create this in our everyday realities, irrespective of the external environment. This is all part of the continuing present moment, creating the next present moment over and over and over again. The momentum of this energy continues creating in the same positive direction.

Even if we find ourselves in challenging situations, by giving thanks, and trusting this is a gift from Divine Wisdom, we can still feel love and gratitude. At this frequency, new opportunities can manifest in this physical realm.

Gratitude for 'High-Lights'

As part of maintaining my focus on gratitude, I always write the 'high-lights' of each day in my journal before I go to sleep. I am constantly amazed that they are usually heart-felt experiences which come from the simplest of life's gifts: conversation and laughter with another person, connecting with nature by looking at a beautiful sunset or sunrise or the visual beauty and scent of a flower. The list becomes endless. They rarely cost anything at all. The more I am grateful for, the more my attitude switches towards one of gratitude. As this is where my energy is focused, then I receive more to be grateful for in my life. The spiral repeats in an ever-expanding, exponential dynamic, growing broader each day.

One of the experiences in life for which I am most grateful was the opportunity to meet with the Dalai Lama. I admire him as an inspirational person and a true leader in this world. He leads by example, encouraging us to rise to our highest aspirations and share them with everyone. He is consistently joyful and light in spirit, irrespective of the hardships that he, personally, and the people of his nation continue to endure.

When His Holiness came to Ireland a couple of years ago, it was nearly impossible to get a ticket but I learned that he would visit a town located less than two hours from my home. I decided to drive there and take my chances to try to see him. Although there was a large crowd of people, as luck would have it, I found myself standing beside an off-duty garda who knew which route the Dalai Lama would take.

When His Holiness came by, the garda kindly moved me forward to meet him. When I stood in front of the Dalai Lama, experiencing a soul-to-soul connection with his beautiful, joyous, smiling eyes, it was once again like merging with the infinite oneness during my NDE. This was one of the most sacred moments in my life. When he saw one large rose and one large quartz crystal in my hands, he kindly blessed them for me and to this day I hold them in my hands during my morning meditations. I know the Buddhist principle of non-attachment should apply to every aspect of our lives. In general, I can detach from material possessions but please don't ask me to give up my blessed meditation crystals!

Gratitude for 'Low-Lights'

I also write my 'Low-Light' in my journal, an issue which is concerning or troubling me. Invariably, as I open up to the lesson from the situation or circumstance, I come to see the gift and learn to give gratitude for this too, though it may take me some time to get there.

By focusing on what we are grateful for with an open heart, we align with our highest thoughts. When we keep our energy at this higher vibration, we continuously create more and more to be grateful for in our lives.

What are you grateful for in your life? Would you consider writing your five High-Lights and your main Low-Light today and every day?

16) EMBRACE YOUR PAST TO CREATE YOUR FUTURE

Do not follow where the path may lead. Go instead where there is no path and leave a trail.
Ralph Waldo Emerson

When we can be grateful for all that we have experienced in our lives, even the most difficult times, then we free ourselves to create the future without any restrictions. So without dwelling on the past, give yourself credit for having overcome adversities and challenges. We can take this to an even deeper level, by giving thanks to our ancestors for all that they have given us and the opportunities that they have made possible in our lives.

❂ ❂ ❂

When I was younger and I learned about the Great Famine in school, it seemed so distant in the past that I never truly understood it until I heard about my own family's history.

My paternal great-grandfather, known as 'Long Tall Tom' (because he grew to be 6 foot 3 inches in height) was born during one of the worst years of the Famine, 1847. He was astounding in many ways. After surviving one of the most calamitous periods of history, he later married and had nine children. My Granny Fitzpatrick, who I recall so well for her own very special energy, was the second youngest of these children.

Granny was only a small child when two of her older siblings boarded the ships for America. She never saw them again, but the family managed to maintain contact through writing letters. Long Tall Tom passed away at the age of 83, an amazing achievement given the harsh conditions during his childhood.

Even more interestingly, Long Tall Tom's father (my great-great grandfather), who was also called Tom, died tragically at the age of 38, either just before his son's birth or shortly thereafter, around 1847. He died of tuberculosis, which was rife in those days due to malnutrition. He left behind his widow and seven young children, all of whom survived to adulthood – challenging the odds, in a most remarkable way, in a time of such population devastation.[36]

When I reflect on what my ancestors endured and overcame in their lives, I am increasingly grateful for the gift of life that they have given me.

What did your ancestors overcome to make your life possible today? What challenges have you overcome to create a better life?

17) GIVE AND RECEIVE

> *Keep love in your heart. A life without it is like a sunless garden when the flowers are dead. The consciousness of loving and being loved brings a warmth and richness to life that nothing else can bring.*

Oscar Wilde

Throughout life, we can often be so focused on material success that we miss the whole point of what life is all about. When we give unconditionally, our hearts open and we naturally become recipients of the infinite love of Universal Consciousness. Giving is one of the greatest ways of opening our hearts. There are many care-givers in society such as nurses, parents and teachers, who through selfless giving in their daily lives, show by example how to live life with an open heart and encourage the best in us.

My family was fortunate when a wonderful woman called Connie appeared in our lives. With her joyful demeanour, she made me smile every time I saw her. Connie was dearly loved by her family, friends and all those who knew her in the village of Howth. In the latter few years of my parents' lives, Connie provided assistance with caring for my mum. She understood the challenges of dealing with Mum's illness, and was exceptionally kind to her. Connie's own mother had also suffered from a similar disease, so she knew how to be loving and compassionate with Mum.

Our family was very grateful for Connie's support throughout the years. After Mum and Dad both passed away, I thanked her from the bottom of my heart for everything that she had done for our family.

Think about the people who inspire the best in you, and give yourself the opportunity to recreate your life anew. Is your heart open to giving and receiving? How can you help others?

18) SUCCESS: TRUE ABUNDANCE

Ordinary riches can be stolen, real riches cannot. In your soul are infinitely precious things that cannot be taken from you.
Oscar Wilde

Life is so fast-paced that we often get caught up in a whirlwind of chaos and lose track of what is really important. At our moment of death, we leave all of our possessions behind and we depart from this planet with either a light-filled and open heart or one that is weighed down and closed. The choice is ours. Material success can be wonderful but true wealth is a state of being. It is an abundance which far exceeds any worldly goods.

When we are truly abundant, we naturally share what we have for the betterment of everyone.

As a child I was lucky to grow up near Howth Castle. The Gaisford-St Lawrence family always kept the gates open to the public, so as children we were able to play on the grounds. To this day, I can still visit and enjoy the beauty of the Neolithic dolmen located at this site because they warmly welcome people to come and enjoy this beautiful place. Even though this tradition of allowing the general public free access to the castle grounds arises from a local legend of the abduction of the heir of the house by the notorious pirate Gráinne Uaile, better known as Grace O'Malley, the fact remains they allow anyone to enter the grounds.[37]

When I was about eight years old, I went on a family holiday to Italy. While waiting for our connecting flight at Heathrow airport in London, I excitedly rode up and down the escalators, which was a treat for me because they were uncommon in Ireland at the time. 'I hope that little brat isn't on our plane,' Eddie Power whispered to his wife, Joan. Eddie and Joan had both met my parents several years earlier, but had not recognised them at the boarding gate. Although a father of three grown-up sons, Eddie did not have much time for children. As it happened, not only were we on the same plane, we were all part of one group, staying in the same hotel in Italy! To everyone's surprise, Eddie's most of all, he and I became fast friends during the vacation. He loved helping me fly my kite on the beach. In retrospect, his offers to help were really a great excuse for him to relive his own joy of flying a kite when he was a boy.

Over the years, Joan, Eddie and I became the best of friends, sharing many happy times together. Then one day, when I was studying in Geneva, I received a call from Mum at the student dorm. 'Eddie passed away unexpectedly from an aortic aneurysm. I will send Joan your love.' After hanging up the receiver, I leaned against the wall, sobbing, as I thought of how all those great times we had shared together were over now.

Even though Joan was 17 years younger than Eddie, and she always knew that he would probably pass first, it was difficult for her to cope after he died. They had been inseparable during their married life. However, she slowly picked herself up after the loss of her beloved Eddie and turned her life around, living to the full for another 21 years.

For the latter few years she lived in a nursing home. Every time I visited her, I was always struck by her joyous attitude to life. She would peer up over her latest novel and exclaim, 'Ah, Róisín, I know who you are!' so proud to remember who I was because at this stage of her life, she knew that her memory was getting weaker. She always squeezed me so tightly when I leaned over to hug her in her chair.

With her hair immaculately groomed and make-up on her face (even though she hardly had a wrinkle well into her eighties), she continued, 'Do you know that I am the luckiest person? I was married to a wonderful man, I have three great sons and I am well cared for here, all the staff treat me so kindly. I get regular physiotherapy, my hair shampooed and set once a week and even drink my gin and tonic at the open bar every Wednesday evening.' On one of those Wednesday evenings, I joined her for a drink. As I poured the tonic into the glass, she winced, 'Wow, girl, hold your whist, for goodness' sakes, don't drown the gin!' She smiled ruefully, quickly interceding to retrieve her drink. Joan never minced her words. More than calling a spade a spade, she called it a shovel and I loved her all the more for this.

Every time I saw her, she always spoke of her beloved Eddie with a soft tenderness in her voice. Although she grieved his passing, she still managed to live with joy as the cornerstone of her life. Some say that grief is the price we pay for loving. Joan taught me that joy is the gift we always receive from a life of shared love.

When I learned that Joan had passed away, I took the day to remember them both by visiting all our old haunts – the Yacht Club in Dún Laoghaire, Finnegan's pub in Dalkey, and the Sorrento drive along the coast south of Dublin. I laughed when I reached the Vico Road as I remembered the day when they had stopped the car and jokingly told me to get out and genuflect outside a particular gate. 'Why?' I had asked inquisitively, and Eddie laughed as he exclaimed, 'That's Bono's house!'

At Joan's funeral, her son Father Frank celebrated the Mass. It was truly a celebration of her life. He quoted

John 10:10, where Jesus said, 'I came that they may have life and have it abundantly.' He encouraged us to live abundantly, not in the material sense, but in terms of fully revelling in every single moment of every day. Joan and Eddie both taught me this greatest of lessons, to truly live life and always be grateful for the blessings. After the funeral, Frank kindly told me that I was the daughter they never had. I will always feel blessed that Eddie and Joan took up with the 'little brat' who was on the plane that day. We shared more than a plane ride together. We shared one truly memorable journey called life.

Love can enter into your life in the most unexpected of ways. Are you open to receiving it? The decision to come from your heart and share your love with others, in your own unique way, is one of the most potent definitions of abundance and success. Are you living your fullest life now? Are you sharing your love with others?

19) TAKE LIFE LIGHTLY

Love the life you live. Live the life you love.
Bob Marley

Whenever we can laugh at ourselves or a situation which is troubling us, in that moment we naturally shift from focusing our energy in a negative direction and turn it towards a positive one. It is impossible to laugh and be angry at the same time. So when we can see the funny side of life, and the positive in every circumstance, we shift the frequency of the energy we emit. It is the same with love – it is impossible to come from fear when we feel love. Being able to overcome our own fears and laugh at ourselves is truly one of life's greatest gifts.

One time, I was speaking with a friend of mine who was struggling with letting go of anger which he had harboured against his brother for decades. Over a six-week period, we talked and talked about this and how, ultimately, it was a choice to let it go. He could not understand this concept and continued wrestling with it in his mind. I knew I had to communicate it in a way that he could hear. My friend is a good-natured person who is loved by his friends for his jovial spirits. So, one day we were out for a drive and while my friend was backing his car into a parking space, as a last-ditch effort, I suddenly turned to him with my face contorted, as if I were fuming with anger and voiced with a raucous growl, 'You too can choose to look and sound just like this when you are angry with your brother.'

He stopped the car so fast I thought I would go through the windshield. He could not stop laughing and sheepishly asked, 'Do I *really* look like that when I am angry – like a cartoon grizzly bear with a sore head?'

I didn't even have to answer him. Finally, he got it in just one sentence. Since then, he told me that whenever he begins to feel angry towards his brother, he now ends up laughing to himself, as he puts the image of the bear square in his mind. As a consequence, the negative energy diffused immensely and he has actually found himself enjoying his brother's company.

Life is so short and valuable. How you do want to live it? How much of your life is lived from the joyful lightness of your heart and how much is lost on unnecessary drama which disconnects you from your deepest truth?

Whenever I find myself in a situation where I am about to embark on a drama, I stop, pull back and evaluate if I really want to go there. Do I want to waste my precious life on unnecessary drama when the alternative of living a great life is available?

I was speaking with a friend of mine one day who was proudly saying how she did not waste her life watching and getting caught up in the drama of the daytime soaps on TV. When I gently suggested to her that her life might be one big cliff-hanging episode after another, with all the drama you could muster, she laughed. On reflection, once she saw how much time she was spending on needless drama, in every area of her life, in her relationships with her family, co-workers and friends, and her choices to constantly repeat the same scenarios day after day and year after year, she decided to re-evaluate her life. She refocused her time and energy on what was really important to her.

Every time she was about to get caught up in more drama, she was able to break the cycle by observing her own behaviour and choosing to respond proactively rather than reactively. By consciously choosing, moment by moment, to centre in her heart, she chose love over fear. As the weeks passed, she was amazed to discover how much extra time she had on her hands, as she was no longer squandering her time and energy in all the dramas. Her life became calmer as she was able to reconnect with her soul at a much deeper level.

If we can have less attachment to drama, situations and outcomes, we can free ourselves to truly live our lives. Also by taking life less seriously, we can remove so many of the invisible shackles associated with the human condition. If we can lighten our spirits by seeing the humour in situations, and laughing at ourselves, then no matter what happens, life can still be a joyous ride filled with many wonderful surprises.

It is our choice how we spend the valuable time we have been given here on earth.

When we can laugh at ourselves and avoid unnecessary drama, life really does become so much lighter. Can you take a lighter look at life?

20) ACCEPTANCE OF IMPERFECTIONS IN LIFE

Reflect on everything; regret nothing.
Michel de Montaigne

Only love is real and I was blessed to truly experience this when I had my NDE. However, the 'reality' of daily life can seem to be chaotic in so many ways: why is this?

When we can recognise that our perfection is found in the so-called imperfections of our day-to-day lives, then we are halfway along the path of healing. Life's trials, travails and tribulations provide us with opportunities to become empowered. By trusting in Divine Wisdom, we can see the truth, and free ourselves to live our lives with compassion instead of judgement. By not attaching to outcomes, we can learn to accept ourselves and embrace the experiences we encounter on this journey.

For example, by accepting the perfection in the imperfection of finding myself in ICU with a brain haemorrhage, and surrendering rather than fighting the situation, I was brought out of my body and merged with the pure love of Universal Consciousness. As a consequence, I was given the most perfect of all gifts because I now experience this love, bliss and joy every day in my life.

It is futile to waste our energy trying to change people in our lives, or certain situations which are beyond our control. The key to unlocking the mystery is to change the thinking within our own minds. By doing this, we reconnect with the truth of who we are, at our deepest soul level. When we can first recognise and then take full responsibility for our own feelings and emotions, then we can see situations with greater clarity.

When we experience feelings or circumstances and cannot understand why certain situations occur, by having the faith to know that there is perfection in the so-called imperfection, we can open ourselves to the healing opportunities which are being presented. As a consequence, we can discover gifts from a deeper, more profound connection with our souls' wisdom. These gifts stay with us as we journey through the rest of our lives.

By trusting that Divine Wisdom creates opportunities for our souls' development, and also in the best interests of all those in our lives, then we can accept the power of healing. No matter what the situation, *love is the answer*. Love comes in many forms but it is always unconditional when given freely with an open heart, and expects nothing in return. True love magnifies the soul and Divine connection.

At times we may find ourselves in situations where we are asked to make decisions which conform to societal convention or make others happy by not rocking the boat, but at our core, we know this is not aligned with our own truths. This is not love but the antithesis of love. We only end up becoming further disconnected from our souls' truths as we lose all sense of ourselves, to the point where we no longer know who we are. And, we have nothing left to give because we have become so empty and depleted.

However, when we are true to ourselves, we become one with the pure love of Universal Consciousness. We radiate this pure love and eternal light. True love is real and open-hearted: it flows in our own best interest and the best interests of everyone in our lives. So give yourself permission to be your radiant self.

Are you embracing the perfection in the imperfections of your life and choosing love? Are you being true to yourself? Are you allowing your radiance to shine?

21) YOUR SOUL'S PRESENCE

I believe that unarmed truth and unconditional love
will have the final word in reality.
  Dr Martin Luther King Jr

The greatest gift we can give to our family, friends and everyone we meet on the journey of life is our souls' full presence. By giving our undivided attention with an open and caring heart, we create the space to share the eternal light. When we emanate this light, we automatically see light in everyone. When we have the courage to live heart-centred lives, then we see that all interactions with other people are opportunities for greater healing from within. The more complete we become, the more we can share love unconditionally with others. Whether we are in the throes of the grieving process (loss of a beloved to death, the end of a relationship or job) or celebrating the joys of life (birth, marriage or new home) sharing our souls' full presence is the greatest gift in every situation.

Being fully present for others is so vitally important during times of loss, especially at the passing of loved ones. After Mum and Dad died, I decided to be on my own for a while to grieve. During this time, Séamus, my old friend from London, came over to see me. He simply said, 'How can I help you, Róisín, what can I do for you?'

He gave me the most precious gift of all – he listened to me with a compassionate heart. He did not try to fix my life; he simply sat and listened as a friend. He allowed me to have a voice and respected whatever I felt, even if he could not understand what I was going through, because up to that point in his life he had never experienced this level of grief.

A couple of years later, his own mother passed away. He always had a strong bond with her, so it was an emotionally challenging time for him. Séamus called over to my home a few months after she had died. I will never forget his comments. 'Róisín, last time I was here just after you lost your parents I hadn't a clue. My goodness, I had no idea what you were going through – the physical exhaustion from grief; the emotional tidal wave that hits you out of the blue when you hear a piece of music or see something that reminds you of your loved one; the sheer panic when you realise that you will never see the people you loved so dearly ever again.'

Taken aback by his candour, I smiled. 'Séamus, you were wonderful – you were truly present with an open heart. It was the best gift you could have given me.' That day, I willingly gave back to Séamus what he had so graciously given to me.

People often feel lost for words at a funeral or in attempting to comfort a grieving friend or family member. I honestly believe the most important gift that we can give is our full presence by showing support and being willing to fully respect all the needs and wishes of the grieving person. We cannot sort their problems or find a solution but we can provide a safe place of compassion.

Everyone grieves loss in their own way and it is so important to respect this. Some people prefer to disappear and quietly be on their own. Others need company to talk through the confounding array of emotions. Some people need a combination of both, or they need them at different times. Whatever a person in grief needs, just listen, be there with an open heart and follow their wishes. It can be such a confusing time because grief cannot be rationalised, categorised or scheduled. Waves of grief can appear when least expected or at the most inopportune moments. Gentle compassion is the greatest gift that we can give to one another.

Through the so-called 'good times and bad times' in life, are you sharing your soul's full presence with everyone in your life?

22) EMBRACE THE FULLNESS OF YOUR SOUL: HEAL ADDICTIONS

Life isn't about finding yourself. Life is about creating yourself.
George Bernard Shaw

When we are born, we lose the conscious connection with the greater part of our souls. It is like a collective amnesia. To heal this pain of separation from our deepest truth, we search endlessly to fill this void. Far too often, rather than taking the path that connects us directly with our souls' truths, we choose short-term relief from the pain of separation. This comes in the form of addictions in various guises. These can include alcohol, drugs, sex, food, over-working, gambling, co-dependent relationships, and addiction to drama. All addictions are fundamentally the same, in the sense that they drain time, energy and resources away from our true path in life. Instead, they channel our energy in a downward spiral. The key is to take responsibility and move forward in the most constructive way possible.[38]

To fully heal from an addiction, it is necessary to deal with the root cause, which is the disconnection from the truth of who we really are. By addressing the addiction, we have an opportunity to deal with this fundamental pain of separation from the soul. If we choose to go into our hearts to heal this pain, we can open ourselves up to the possibility of regaining this soul connection.

On reflection, when I was younger, I was a workaholic. I worked in order to run away from my own inner fears and insecurities. Although in the short term, it seemed to provide relief from my pain, in the long term, because I was gradually disconnecting from my soul's truth, I created unnecessary pain. The harder I worked, the more disconnected I became until eventually I stopped, or to be more accurate, I was physically unable to go any further when I developed CFS. However, once I chose to go within, moment to moment, I learned to reconnect with my heart and truth at a deeper soul level. This was then magnified intensely when I experienced the NDE.

Thus by consciously choosing to face my pain, I was able to break the cycle. This was a huge opportunity to heal and unify with my soul. When we recognise that our true essence is pure love because each and every one of us is created from the love of Universal Consciousness, then we gain the freedom to live our best lives.

The opportunity is always presented to you to reconnect with your soul. Are you choosing to heal yourself by coming from your heart and the fullness of your soul?

23) CHOOSE YOUR THOUGHTS TO CHANGE YOUR FEELINGS

> *The greatest discovery of my generation is that a human being can alter his life by altering his attitudes.*
>
> William James

The thoughts we think have a powerful and direct correlation with the emotions we feel. We can actually change our feelings about situations or circumstances in life, depending on the thoughts we choose. A friend of mine took this to heart and this was his experience.

One day, when he was in a crowded airport waiting for a plane, a loud, irritating voice droned on relentlessly over the PA system. My friend admitted that this grated on every nerve in his body, as the announcer broadcast all flight arrivals and departures. There was no escape. He had to sit and wait until he could board his flight. It seemed like an eternity, with the incessant noise blaring in his ears.

He decided that as there was nowhere for him to go, rather than feeling frustrated about the external circumstances over which he had no control, he chose to change his thoughts from within. To his amazement, the idea then came to him to imagine a scenario. What if the announcer were deaf and mute all his life, and that very day he had been given the gifts of hearing and speech? Instantaneously, my friend felt overcome by compassion and joy for this person. From then on, he actually even enjoyed hearing the announcer's voice. So what had changed? The only difference was my friend's perception of the situation.

Thus, by changing how we think, we can affect our feelings and therefore also how we act in every situation. If we make the decision to choose only loving thoughts, we can create loving feelings and experience more love in our lives. Yes, that can at times be a difficult choice. By the same token, it is not necessary to wait for situations to trigger negative emotions. We have the choice to always approach everyone we meet and the circumstances we encounter in our lives with an attitude of love and compassion.

What thoughts are you generally thinking? Do they come from love?

24) THE GIFT OF LIFE

I wish I could show you, when you are lonely or in darkness, the astonishing light of your own being.
Hafiz

Since I've been sharing my art over the years at exhibitions and talks, many people have expressed their feelings to me of not belonging here. They have told me that their experience of life can be challenging because there is so much violence portrayed every day. If we can shift our perspective to see that love is our true essence, then we can be in this world, but not limited by the mental perceptions of this world. With the knowledge and belief that our core truth is love, it is possible to be at peace within, irrespective of the external circumstances.

We are here in our physical bodies now. This is where we belong for this moment in time.

Each one of us has been given the gift of life. By acknowledging this gift of life, and even revelling in all the possibilities open to us throughout this journey, we can appreciate the true worth of our own lives. Unfortunately, some people have become 'invisible' because they do not conform to society's definitions of being worthy, or we ourselves do not recognise our own worthiness. If we could come from our hearts with love, we would recognise the importance of every single person's life, irrespective of where they were born on this planet. The lives of the young, elderly, disabled, people

of different races, genders, sexual orientation, classes
and cultures would be considered all equal in value. We
would also recognise the importance of our own lives.

◉ ◉ ◉

When I was practising as a homeopath, an elderly
gentleman used to visit me regularly. He had worked for
over 60 years, and was obviously used to being active,
with a purpose in life. However, since his retirement I
watched him becoming visibly older and more fragile on
all levels. A few months after he retired, I remember one
day when we were sitting in my practice room he stared
out the window overlooking the sea. He seemed quite
down in himself, which was unusual because he was
generally in great spirits. As we spoke, he said, 'Róisín,
I don't have anything to contribute anymore and I feel
like a nuisance. I am an old man and life is too fast-paced
for me, I cannot keep up. It takes me so much longer to
do everything that my whole day is busy, yet nothing is
done.' He explained that the young and the elderly are
marginalised by society and that was how he was feeling
since he had retired.

I was dumbfounded. How could this wonderful man,
whom I knew to be the bedrock of his family, actually
be thinking this way? I also saw that society is so ageist.
As a man, feeling that he was no longer contributing,
even though he had worked for three quarters of his
life and created a business that gave so many clients
joy and employees a livelihood, he felt that he had no

further purpose. I listened attentively to understand what he was feeling and shared with him how much he was loved by his family. We also focused on other ways that he could find more meaning in life. As we worked together over the next few months, thankfully he turned the corner as he found new ways to enjoy life.

After he left on that particular day, I reflected on our discussion and realised the huge wake-up call this man had given me. I saw that I had inadvertently become so caught up in the speed of living that I was missing out on what was really important in life. By refocusing on coming from my heart, and sharing love, which is truly all that matters, I was blessed to be able to share this with my own parents for more than a decade before they passed away. This time together became a wonderful opportunity to really get to know my parents for who they were, with all of their dreams and hopes, and to simply enjoy each other's company. Some of our best times together were during those years.

One evening, a few months before Dad passed away, a friend of mine came over to my parents' home. Dad walked in from the kitchen carrying a tray in his arms, with a freshly brewed pot of tea and sliced fruit cake. He sat down at the table and began chatting with us. We stayed up for hours, as he recalled old memories from when he was younger. We listened as he reminisced about the Zeppelin flying overhead *en route* to America. He would have been about five years old at the time. My friend and I could see him becoming that little boy again as he stared up at the ceiling in awe reliving the experience of the gigantic airship filling the sky overhead. He also remembered when he borrowed his sister's ice-skates and skated on a frozen lake. He laughed because they were too small for him but he was determined to wear them anyway and skate over the ice with great freedom. He also recounted many other tales, including his memory of when the Second World War started. He described how saddened he felt when he later learned that some of his classmates from school were killed after they became fighter pilots in the war. He replayed his lucky strokes from many of the golf championships in which he competed. He gave us advice from his golfing days: 'Always focus on the present moment and give whatever you are doing your best shot.'

You have the choice to fully appreciate this gift of life. Are you embracing the gifts of wisdom and love that others are giving to you? Are you living your fullest life now? Are you sharing your love with others? Are you giving life your best shot?

25) SOUL'S LOVING PERSPECTIVE

You are a child of God. You were created in a blinding flash of creativity, a primal thought when God extended himself.
Marianne Williamson

Have you ever had the experience of being in the presence of someone who looks through the eyes of love? It is as if their eyes can light up the room. They make you feel alive, vibrant, filled with possibility and potential. You feel like you can take on the world. In the presence of such people you tap into your soul's potential because they are flowing and overflowing with their soul's light.

On the other hand, have you ever had the experience of being in someone's company when you feel your life-blood draining from you? It feels as if everything is sucked out, until you are left lifeless, limp – nothing but an empty shell. Although this is not conscious, their modus operandi is 'What can I take?' instead of 'What can I give?' In these situations, if we can consciously choose to stay at the frequency of love and compassion for everyone involved, then we can still remain empowered.

We are each responsible for what we share with each other and radiate in this world. If we choose, we can allow the unconditional love of Universal Consciousness to flow through us in a way that enhances our lives and also enhances the lives of those we touch, in an equally loving way. By loving our neighbour as ourselves, not more than, not less than, but equally, we create the space for unconditional love to pour into every interaction and relationship in our lives.[39]

If we choose to look at every relationship through loving eyes then we can see each encounter with another person as an opportunity for Divine healing. Whether the interaction is with a shopkeeper, an insurance broker or a family member, whether the person is in our lives for three minutes, three years or 30 years, every time we can view the relationship from this perspective, we open ourselves to receiving the greatest of gifts. By releasing any accumulated negative emotions and thoughts which dim our souls' light, we strengthen our souls' connection. As a result, we become clearer, with a more profound connection to Universal Consciousness. If we choose to open ourselves to receiving this Divine Grace, then it floods into every cell of our beings, every moment of our lives and into every relationship.

How do you make the transition to view, through the lens of love, the perspective of your soul?

During my NDE this was automatic. It was all that existed. It was real. It was the truth. It was the only way of seeing and perceiving. Yet, at the human level, when we get caught up in day-to-day 'reality', it can seem so elusive. If we can become able to view all the challenging situations in life from this angle, then the dross falls away and a clear path appears.

So let's imagine, you are with someone who loves you unconditionally. It can be someone living or someone who has already passed on. In your mind's eye, simply imagine yourself in the presence of this person. It could be one of your parents, or grandparents, or maybe a favourite aunt, uncle, teacher or neighbour – choose someone special who always loves you. Allow yourself to see all aspects of your life, including any challenging situations, *through their eyes.*

You know that this person loves you unconditionally and would not want you to dwell, even for a moment, on negative thoughts and emotions which hurt you. They want the best for you. By taking this step back from the details of the circumstances in your life, and looking at them through the lens of unconditional love, you will find that all the negative thoughts and emotions simply fade away. Clarity of thought emanates from this loving compassion. This is the soul's vision. This is the truth. This is your pathway forward.

From this perspective, you may find yourself receiving guidance if you go still and listen to your inner voice, or you may see signs as you go about your daily life. If you allow yourself to be open to these synchronistic messages, you will receive more and more of them, showing you how to handle various situations in your life, all the while maintaining focus on creating your best life.

It is a blessing to have the experience of being in the presence of someone who lives life this way, always seeing everyone and everything through loving eyes. These people seem to radiate an intangible yet, paradoxically, highly tangible light. There is nothing more special than 'seeing' and experiencing this light as it radiates out to envelop everyone. All you have to do is walk into the room and you immediately feel surrounded by the loving glow.

We can all choose to see this world through the loving eyes of love. If we do this, we open the door to gaining a much clearer perspective on life. If we can move away from the rigid, constrained thinking of our minds towards the more fluid, spontaneous feeling in our hearts, we can lighten up and flow with life.

Do you have people in your life who love you unconditionally? Are you choosing to look at everyone in your life through loving eyes? Are you loving your family, friends, neighbours, work colleagues, not more than, not less than, but equally, as you love yourself?

Conscious Living and Dying

The best and most beautiful things in the world cannot be seen or even touched. They must be felt with the heart.
Helen Keller

If we choose to navigate life consciously, we can make the journey easier and more enjoyable for ourselves and for everyone we encounter on the way.

Conscious Awareness of Illness

In modern Western society, we tend to shun illness. Yet, when we go through challenging times during our lives, if we can simply be present, as opposed to judging and running away from the circumstances, we often begin to see beauty in the experiences.

I remember one day, when I was physically weak with CFS, my sister had kindly driven me to the optician's to get a new pair of glasses. As I slumped in the chair, wrapped up in my black woollen coat, I was unable to hold myself upright due to my physical weakness and I felt totally down in the dumps, pitying myself. When I looked up, I saw a young man, in his mid-teens, sitting in a specialised wheelchair. He was a quadriplegic. His mother lovingly adjusted his new spectacles on his face for him. The only part of his body that he could move were the muscles in his face, and boy did he use them! A spirit lit up, radiating through his eyes as joy beamed all over his face. I became so ashamed of my own self-pitying and resolved to focus on all the things to be grateful for in my life.

This young man inspires me to this day. Whenever I feel a bit down in myself or tired, I always think of him and his courage against the odds, his infectious laughter and his powerful, magnetic presence. The great irony is that society may categorise him as being less than able because of his physical infirmity, but he had a potent spiritual presence, an eternal light, which outshone that of most 'healthy' people.

Conscious Awareness of Living

Years ago, I read an inspiring story about a community of women in Senegal, West Africa. Their example of resilience shows that *the answers always lie within*. And, one of the greatest gifts we can give to one another is the gift of empowerment, to encourage each other to hear this quiet, yet powerful, inner voice.

Lynne Twist describes in her book *The Soul of Money* how, as a professional fundraiser, she travelled the world both receiving money from those who wished to donate and distributing these finances to assist various projects around the globe.[40] On one occasion her work brought her deep into the Sahel Desert in Senegal. She had heard about the challenges facing a small tribal community living in a remote village. These people had been negatively affected by the expansion of the desert and its encroachment onto their land over the previous years.

In the scorching heat, with grains of pale orange sand swirling in the air making it difficult to breathe, they drove for several hours until there were no signs of vegetation or any form of life in this stark and windswept landscape. Lynne Twist wondered how anyone could survive in such a forsaken place. Guided by a compass, they drove in the open desert until they heard drumming in the distance. As they approached, it became louder until they saw small children running towards the cars. In stark contrast with the inhospitable landscape, these boys and girls were exuberant with *joie de vivre*.

While seeking shelter under two large baobab trees from the scorching heat and sand-laden wind, the men, women and children began dancing and clapping in an enthusiastic celebration to welcome the visitors. After a while the men, who were obviously the leaders of the community, huddled in a circle and explained how they were struggling to survive because of the scarcity of water. Yet the desert was still their spiritual home and they wished to find a way to be able to stay there.

In this society, the men voiced the opinions and were empowered to speak for everyone. However, the women were the key to the solution because they instinctively knew that there was an underground lake. They did not need money or food from Lynne Twist and her organisation. All they required from her was to arrange with the elders that the women could have permission to dig a well deep enough to search for this water, and some basic tools to assist them with this project. Once this was organised, the women eagerly set about their task and within a year they found the source of water. They also constructed a pumping system and water tower for storage. This water served not only their village but 17 other villages, transforming this region of Senegal into a hub of activity with flourishing families, schools and businesses.

Through their determination and dignity, these women show us how the answers always lie within. When we empower each other to listen to our souls' guidance, we tap into the Source, the well-spring from which all knowledge is obtained. The answers flow not only for our highest good, but also in the best interest of the greater community.

If we consciously choose to tap into our own loving light and share this with every person we encounter, in every moment of every day on this journey of life, then we are living our souls' purpose of being and sharing the eternal light. As we become attuned to this light, our energy changes, affecting other people, creating ripple effects out into the world.

Conscious Awareness of Death

In our Western society we tend to shy away from looking

at death. We become obsessed with 'surviving' and 'saving lives at all cost', implying that death is a failure. By dying, we have somehow 'lost the battle' or have 'given up'. Yet, from my experience of the NDE, I believe that each and every one of us is always part of the *solas síoraí* – eternal light – whether we are here in physical form, wearing a suit of bones and muscles, or whether we have passed on beyond this material realm and merged more fully with our souls' essence. We don't know when the moment of our death is fated to be, but we can choose, moment to moment, how we live our lives.

When I had my NDE, I certainly did not see death as a failure. I learned that there is a much larger perspective on life and death. We are all born for a purpose. With our free will, we either positively or negatively impact the lives of others depending on the choices that we make. Each moment is an opportunity to integrate more of our souls' loving light while we live here on earth. When our time is up, we pass from this physical realm, into the eternal realm of light. Similarly, when someone dear to us passes away, we have the choice to focus on the moment of their death and the loss, or to see the beauty of their life and all that they contributed and can still contribute in non-material ways.

Conscious Awareness of the Soul

Through the centuries, our interpretation of God has often been one of a Divine father figure, with man created in this patriarchal image.[41]

This emphasis on the physical nature of the resemblance between God and man has been reflected in numerous religious creeds, and depicted regularly in famous artworks such as Michelangelo's fresco in the Sistine Chapel.

What if we choose not to limit ourselves to such a human likeness of God, and to open ourselves to a deeper, more expanded spiritual perspective as well?

Then we could see God as an infinite expanse of Divine Light and this impermanent world would simply be an extension of the eternal light.[42] In this latter scenario, to create man in the image of God would have very different results. We would go far beyond just our bodily form to fully embrace the light within each of our souls. We would see ourselves as a manifestation of this light, with the gift of the Divine spark of light deep within our humanity.

During my NDE I experienced myself as pure light, surrounded by a blissful, loving light which was Divine in every way. I knew from that moment on that my physicality was derived from my spiritual essence. I also understood that it was not necessary to undergo an NDE, or similar spiritual crisis, to open up to our essence. This Divine Light is our deepest truth. If we can expand our understanding of our image of God to fully embrace this Divine Light, then we can learn to see ourselves as luminous beings originating from a vast expanse of loving light.

From this perspective, we can see that we are temporarily 'born' in this material world as human forms, and then return at the moment of 'death' to the infinite oneness of Universal Consciousness.

At the level of the soul, everyone is equal. We originate from the same Source energy. Thus, there is no categorisation of 'better than' or 'worse than', which would imply a differentiation. When we see this truth, it makes life so simple, as it does not matter a jot where you were born, the social class in which you were reared, your age, your gender or your level of education. We are all equal, coming from eternal light and returning to the same eternal light, without having to bring our passports, university diplomas, house or car keys with us!

The only difference is *how* we choose to live our lives. Instead of blaming a Divine being (whom perhaps we have limited by our human interpretation) for the calamities and tragedies in this world, we have the opportunity to recognise that we are all one with this eternal light, and share our energy to co-create our collective experiences on this planet.

If we choose to recognise our connection with the Divine Wisdom of eternal light, we can create beauty even in the most challenging of circumstances and contribute to society by making a difference in the lives of others. Or, if we have forgotten the truth of who we really are, we become disconnected from this Source and unconsciously behave in ways which drain energy from others, by seeking to take control of external circumstances.

By choosing to tap into the eternal light, we automatically radiate this light, as it naturally flows through us. We can live with loving compassion and clarity of purpose, sharing this light with everyone we meet on life's journey. By remembering the truth of who we really are, we can rejoice and delight in each other's light. If we can remain steadfast in our focus on the light, amazing results can be achieved.

Conclusion

We are all meant to shine; we were born to make manifest the glory of God that is within us. As we let our light shine, we unconsciously give other people permission to do the same. As we are liberated from our own fear, our presence automatically liberates others.[43]

Marianne Williamson

By having faith, we can experience the pure love of Universal Consciousness. It is sometimes challenging to have the faith to see and believe, yet this loving light does exist. It exists in each and every one of us, if we choose to connect within. As we individually make the choice to journey into the depths of our souls and tap into this light, we can transform our own lives and, in doing so, we can share this light with everyone we touch during our brief lifetime.

As we integrate the greater part of our souls into our physical beings, we become stronger beacons for sharing this light. All of this takes faith to believe in a Universal Consciousness with which we co-create our lives, wisdom to listen to the guidance and courage to act on these messages. Then we are shown how to follow or even create a whole new path aligned with our deepest truths and highest calling.

The Divine Wisdom of Universal Consciousness has everything ready and waiting for you to fulfil your soul's desires and aspirations.

The question is: are you ready?

My Wishes for You

> There is a place that you are to fill and no one else can fill, something you are to do, which no one else can do.
> Plato

I wish for you to experience your soul's truth of pure love. *The most precious gift that you can give to yourself is the realisation that you are pure love.* You are a physical expression of Universal Consciousness, which is pure love. The understanding and mastery of self-love is the key to creating your best life.

I wish for you to embrace your radiance and enjoy life by following your passion. Life can be an amazing adventure, filled with awe and wonder, if you allow it to magically unfold before you.

I wish for you to have the courage to grow and expand into the fullness of your soul, and to seize the moment, by choosing love over fear.

I wish for you to allow yourself to 'feel love and radiate light,' for 'Heaven' is a state of being that lies within you.

I wish for you to take the leap of faith and live your soul's grandest vision, by following your heart's desires. By making the shift from surviving to thriving, you can confidently move towards creating, attaining and living the life of your dreams.

I wish for you to step into your destiny and share your unique talents and gifts in a way that enhances the lives of others.

I wish for you, during your brief lifetime here on earth, to be empowered by your knowledge of the eternal light.

I also wish, at the moment of your death, for you to pass with ease through the illusory veil, to fully merge and become one with the pure love of Universal Consciousness and experience the beauty of the eternal light – *solas síoraí*.

As we all change, one by one, moment by moment, and choose to connect with Universal Consciousness, allowing unconditional love to flow through us, the whole planet will be transformed. Every life will be recognised to have equal value at the level of the soul, and be seen to be inextricably linked with the lives of everyone else on this planet. Nature and the environment will be respected. Money will be invested in creating peace on earth. As each person awakens from the collective amnesia of who we really are at a soul level, miraculous solutions will be found for the highest good of all humankind.

Cherish your visions; cherish your ideals, cherish the music that stirs in your heart, the beauty that forms

> *in your mind, the loveliness that drapes your purest*
> *thoughts, for out of them will grow all delightful*
> *conditions, all heavenly environment; of these, if you*
> *remain true to them, your world will at last be built.*

James Allen[44]

EPILOGUE

As you journey on this path, I wish you safe travels in finding your unique way.

May the blessing of light be on you, light without and light within.[45]

I wish for you to love your life, radiate your light and enjoy every precious moment of 'Heaven' here on earth.

With love,
Róisín

ENDNOTES

1. When we met, I asked Dr Greyson how he first came to study near death experiences. He explained that he became involved in this field in 1975, when he was the medical supervisor for a young intern by the name of Raymond Moody. Dr Moody had recently published a book called *Life After Life*, which coined the phrase 'near death experience'. Within a few months, it became an international best seller and as a result of the success of his book, Dr Moody was inundated with thousands of personal letters from people describing their own NDEs. He asked Dr Greyson to assist him with analysing all these letters. They soon realised that there was virtually no acknowledgement of NDEs, let alone research being performed by the medical profession. This is how the research on NDEs began in the United States. Drs Greyson and Moody understood that the reason the medical profession was not hearing about patients' NDEs was because the vast majority of physicians had never heard of such a phenomenon. Consequently, they never thought to ask their patients who had been in life-threatening situations whether they had experienced an NDE.

   Dr Greyson explained that, as is often the case when breaking ground in medical research, it took a lot of courage to speak about this topic in the scientific community decades ago, and to bring this to the attention of the general public. Since then, Drs Moody and Greyson and many other medical professionals have dedicated their lives to understanding the enigma of NDEs and of life beyond death. In particular, they have focused on how the mind and consciousness are not limited by the physical structure of the brain.

2. Note to reader: while there are many definitions of the following terms in various bodies of literature, from the religious to the philosophical, I offer my own definitions for the purpose of clarity in this book. I define 'soul' as the spark of Divine Light at the very essence of our beings and it is also an integral part of the pure love of Universal Consciousness. I understand Universal Consciousness to be the primordial creator of life, the Source energy from which each and every one of us and all of creation originates. This energy is the purest form of absolute, unconditional love.

3. According to archaeologist Helen Roche, this portal tomb dates from approximately 3600 BC, the Neolithic (New Stone Age) period.

   Howth is featured in local folklore and some of the legendary tales. The dolmen was described as an entrance to the 'Otherworld' because it was believed to be a dwelling place of the supernatural, luminous deities known as the *Tuatha Dé*. Áed was the king of this mythical otherworldly mound and Étaín was his beautiful fair-haired daughter. After she refused a proposal of marriage offered by the son of the King of Ireland, she chose to marry Oscar, a grandson of the infamous warrior Finn. Oscar was a renowned champion in his own right. With his stalwart courage he was often portrayed as a triumphant hero playing the foremost role in battle. Tragically, Oscar lost his life in combat when a spear pierced his heart, and his wife Étaín died of a broken heart, grieving the loss of her husband. In this legend, Étaín was buried under the great dolmen, thus returning to the eternal 'Otherworld'. Oscar's persona allegedly survived death, and often came to the assistance of his comrades in times of need. *Tales of the Elders of Ireland*, translated by Ann Dooley and Harry Roe, Oxford University Press (1999), pp. 158–60.

4. Oppenheimer, A.R., *IRA: The Bombs and the Bullets: A History of Deadly Ingenuity*, Irish Academic Press (2009), p. 124.

5. De Baróid, Ciarán, *Ballymurphy: The Irish War*, Pluto Press (2000), p. 325. The Baltic Exchange was extensively damaged and later razed to the ground. This is now the location of London's famous 'Gherkin' building.

6. The bomb caused one fatality and 44 injuries.

7. English, Richard, *Armed Struggle: The History of the IRA*, Pan Books (2000), p. 296.
8. Swift, Jonathan, *Gulliver's Travels*, Bloomsbury Books (1993, first published 1735).
9. 'God is merely the love within us, so returning to Him is a return to ourselves.' Williamson, Marianne, *A Return to Love*, HarperCollins (1992), p. 52.
10. Angiogram: a procedure where dye is injected so that blood vessels show up clearly on X-ray or fluoroscopy. This procedure is used to see where there are problems with circulation, including aneurysms and haemorrhages.
11. My medical notes stated: 'CT brain showed acute haemorrhage in basal cistern, anterior to brainstem, mainly right-sided.'
12. My medical records from both St Columcille's Hospital and Beaumont Hospital (the Irish centre for excellence in brain trauma) verify the occurrence of a subarachnoid brain haemorrhage on 22 March 2004.
13. The NDE I experienced was ranked higher than average on the definitive NDE verification scale, developed by Dr Bruce Greyson. When I met Dr Greyson, he confirmed my experience. He explained that NDEs occur in life-threatening situations; traumatic events such as the brain haemorrhage that I experienced qualified as a cause for an NDE. The post-NDE experiences were also verified, as part of the whole NDE. He explained that these are a common phenomenon. They serve the purpose of assisting the NDE experiencer to integrate the huge shift in consciousness which occurs as a result of the NDE. They help the person to readjust to life again after the shock and also the wonderful revelations about life and death experienced during the NDE. These post-NDE experiences provide an explanation, a sort of template or framework, for understanding the connection with Universal Consciousness. They help to make sense of the transformational power of the NDE and show how to integrate this energy going forward in life. In addition, review of my medical records shows that at the time of the NDE, I was not under the influence of any medication at a dosage that induces hallucinations or affects cognitive function. This was confirmed by Dr Greyson. It is an important point because some medicines can cause vivid dreams or hallucinations which can be misinterpreted as 'out-of-body' or near death experiences. For further information please read, 'Differentiating Spiritual and Psychotic Experiences', Dr Greyson, *Journal of Near-Death Studies*, 32 (3), Spring 2014.

14. Although this blessing was probably written in more recent centuries, there are many Biblical references in the medieval texts to God holding the world in his hand. Please see Carey, John, *King of Mysteries: Early Irish Religious Writings*, Four Courts Press (2000), pp. 41, 94.

15. *May the road rise up to meet you,*
    May the wind be always at your back,
    May the sun shine warm upon your face,
    And rains fall soft upon your fields,
    And until we meet again,
    May God hold you in the palm of His hand.

16. Yeats, W.B., *I Am of Ireland: Favorite Poems by W.B. Yeats*, Gill & Macmillan (2010), p. 89.

17. In the English language, the origins for 'Good bye' are 'God be with you' (Oxford English Dictionary). 'A-Dieu' in French may also have a similar etymology.

18. Dalai Lama quoted in Sogyal Rinpoche, *The Tibetan Book of Living and Dying*, Random House (1998), foreword.

19. For further information please see Dr Raymond Moody, *Glimpses of Eternity: An Investigation into Shared Death Experiences*, Random House (2010). At the time of this phenomenon occurring I had never heard of such an experience. I learned about it a few years later while researching this book.

20. Interestingly, *lux aeterna*, the Latin for 'eternal light', was used in Christian Requiem Masses in medieval times, to wish eternal peace, rest and light to the deceased. In Judaism, a lamp situated above the ark in every synagogue is known as the 'eternal light'. This light burns continuously as a symbol of God's eternal presence and of the covenant with God.

21. In Dineen's Irish Dictionary the term for a wake is *tórramh aingeal* (pronounced *thor-av angle*), meaning 'an escort of angels', by the poet Pádraigín Haicéad (1604–54).

22. Betty Cosgrave has written a beautiful inspiring book titled *The Whispering Soul*, IPPS (2009).

23. Eye Movement Desensitisation and Reprocessing (EMDR) is a psychotherapy which enables people to heal from the symptoms and emotional distress resulting from challenging life experiences. Repeated studies show that, by using EMDR, people can quickly experience healing benefits. EMDR incorporates right-left bilateral eye movements, undulating bilateral sound, or right-left body tapping, along with a body-centred protocol. Bilateral

stimulation of the brain promotes communication between its two hemispheres, facilitating access to the unconscious and making rapid change possible.

24. The third verse of the Book of Genesis in the King James Bible reads:

1:1 In the beginning God created the Heaven and the earth.

1:2 And the earth was without form, and void; and darkness was upon the face of the deep. And the Spirit of God moved upon the face of the waters.

1:3 And God said, Let there be light: and there was light.

25 I am not an academician in either archaeology or the ancient legends of Ireland, but I have a passion to understand this heritage and as such have extensively researched the history and culture of Ireland. I reference various sources of information, from some of the older writings to the more modern interpretations, to give a broad understanding of these subjects. In the acknowledgements of this book I express my gratitude to those individuals whose work has led me to a greater understanding of these areas.

26. Yeats, W.B., from the poem 'Under Ben Bulben', quoted in *I Am of Ireland: Favorite Poems by W.B. Yeats*, Gill & Macmillan (2010), p. 146.

27. For more information about the Bard Summer School, please see www.bard.ie

28. Although the particulars of the various tribes are open to question, the stories from the 'Mythological Cycle' reflect the constant flow of immigration and emigration of different waves of ethnic groups throughout the millennia. Gantz, Jeffrey, *Early Irish Myths and Sagas*, Penguin Books (1981), p. 6.

29. Eoin MacNeill quotes in T.F. O'Rahilly, *Early Irish Mythology*, Dublin Institute for Advanced Studies (1976, first published 1946), p. 482; d'Arbois de Jubainville, quoted in ibid., p. 264; Carey, John, 'The Baptism of the Gods', in *A Single Ray of the Sun*, Celtic Studies Publications (2011), p. 33; MacKillop, James, *Oxford Dictionary of Celtic Mythology*, Oxford University Press (2004, first published 1998), p. 197; Gregory, Lady Augusta, *Complete Irish Mythology*, preface by W.B. Yeats, Bounty Books (reprinted 2005), p. 61 (originally published by John Murray Publishers with the titles *Gods and Fighting Men* (1904) and *Cuchulain of Muirthemne* (1902)); Carey, John, 'Time, Memory and the Boyne Necropolis', *Proceedings of the Harvard Celtic Colloquium*, 10 (1993), pp. 24–30; Ó hÓgáin, Dáithí, *The Lore of Ireland: An Encyclopedia of Myth, Legend and Romance* (2006), p. 478. Carey, John, '*Tuath Dé*', in Koch, John, *Celtic Culture: A Historical Encyclopedia* (2006), Vol. V, pp. 1,693–6.

30. The names of some of the Otherworlds are as follows: 'Land of Youth', *Tír na nÓige* (pronounced *teer na no-igue*); 'Land of the Living', *Tír na mBeó* (pronounced *teer na may-oh*); 'Delightful Plain', *Mag Mell* (pronounced *moy mell*); 'Land of Promise', *Tír Tairngire* (pronounced *teer tahrn-ir-i*); 'Land of Light', *Tír na Sorcha* (pronounced *teer na sore-ka*); 'Plain of Two Mists', *Mag Da Chéo* (pronounced *moy da key-o*); 'Silver Cloud Land'; and 'Land of Bliss'. Carey, John, 'The Location of the Otherworld in Irish Tradition,' in J. Wooding (ed.), *The Otherworld Voyages in Early Irish Literature*, Four Courts Press (2000), p. 115; Joyce, P.W., *A Social History of Ancient Ireland*, Vol. I, Gill & Sons (1920), pp. 293–6; Dames, Michael, *Ireland: A Sacred Journey*, Element Books (2000), p. 73.

    Tír na nÓg actually means 'the Land of the Young Ones'. It has become the most familiar form because of its use in the famous eighteenth-century poem about Oisín and Niamh, but is in fact a relatively rare variant on the much more common *Tír na hÓige* (Land of Youth). *Tír na mBeó* (Land of the Living) and *Tír Tairngire* (Promised Land) are both terms taken originally from the Bible, which illustrates the important influence which Christian ideas of Heaven and paradise had on Irish conceptions of the happy Otherworld. *Tír na Sorcha* (Land of Light) is found in late texts and oral wonder tales and it may refer to a land somewhere in the imagined East, sometimes identified with Syria, rather than a native Otherworld *per se*. 'Silver Cloud Land' is a name found only in the wonderful tale *The Voyage of Bran*. This detailed information about the Otherworlds was kindly provided by John Carey.

31. John Moriarty (2006), p. 10.

32. This is one possible etymological source for leprechaun, with *Lu-chorpán* meaning 'little Lugh body'. MacKillop, James, *Oxford Dictionary of Celtic Mythology* (2004), p. 306. See also Bisagni, Jacopo, 'Leprechaun: A New Etymology', *Cambrian Medieval Celtic Studies*, 64 (winter, 2012), pp. 47–84 for alternative etymological origins of this word.

33. MacCana, Proinsias, *Celtic Mythology* (1968), p. 65. According to John Carey (via correspondence), the oldest reference to the people of the *sídh* that we have is in Tírechán's late seventh-century account of Patrick, describing them as 'earthly gods' (*dei terreni*). See also 'The supernatural inhabitants of Ireland [are] the immortal beings variously designated by such phrases as *Tuatha Dé* 'tribes of god' or *aes side* 'people of the Otherworld mounds', from John Carey, 'Time, Memory and the Boyne Necropolis', *Proceedings of the Harvard Celtic Colloquium*, Vol. 10 (1993), presented at the Tenth Harvard Celtic Colloquium, p. 24.

The word *sí* (*síd* or *sídhe*) has a couple of meanings in Irish. *Sí* refers to the stone mounds which were considered to be the residences of the immortal beings and places where the 'Otherworld' could be accessed. It also refers to the supernatural spirits, more recently known as the fairies, who inhabit these mounds. Thus, the term refers to both the sites and their ethereal inhabitants, hence the colloquial name 'fairy mound'. Please see MacCana, Proinsias, *Celtic Mythology* (1968), p. 65; Murphy, Gerard, *Saga and Myth in Ancient Ireland,* published for the Cultural Relations Committee of Ireland (1955), p. 14; Ó hÓgáin, Dáithí, *The Sacred Isle: Belief and Religion in Pre-Christian Ireland* (1999), p. 105; Thompson, Tok, 'Clocha Geala/Clocha Uaisle: White Quartz in Irish Tradition', *Béaloideas: Journal of the Folklore of Ireland Society*, Vol. 73 (2005), p. 111; Evans-Wentz, W.Y., *The Fairy Faith in Celtic Countries,* The Lost Library, Glastonbury, first published by Henry Frowde (1911), p. 284. Interestingly, in addition to the meanings stated above, *síd* also means 'peace' (Carey, John (1999), p. 29); Ó Cathasaigh, Tomás, *'The Semantics of Síd'*, Égise, xvii (1978), pp. 137–55.

34. The depth to which the light penetrates the cairn also shifts, with the peak occurring around the time of the solstice. Moroney, Anne-Marie, *Dowth: Winter Sunsets*, Flaxmill Publications (2002), pp.11–14.

35. Archaeologist Robert Hensey presents the idea that Neolithic man may have been interested in observing the solar phenomena over a period of time around certain key turning points in the year: 'Creating an alignment may not have been an end in itself; instead, it may have been a means to witness and engage with a natural phenomenon in a controlled ritual context. The construction of an astronomically aligned chambered cairn would have allowed this engagement to happen in a much more focused way than would have ordinarily been the case.' Hensey, Robert, 'The Observance of Light: A Ritualistic Perspective on "Imperfectly" Aligned Passage Tombs', *Time and Mind: The Journal of Archaeology, Consciousness and Culture*, Vol. 1, No. 3 (November 2008), p. 325.

36. Ireland's Great Famine ranks among the worst tragedies of nineteenth-century Europe. Between 1845 and 1850, approximately 1.5 million Irish men, women and children died of starvation or related diseases. By 1855, more than 2 million had emigrated to avoid a similar fate. Source: Ireland's Great Hunger Museum, Quinnipiac University, Hamden, CT.

37. According to the tale, around 1575, after returning from a

visit with Queen Elizabeth I, Grace O'Malley landed in Howth, intending to dine with the Lord of the castle. Upon her arrival, she found the gates of the castle closed, prohibiting her entry. Indignant at this breach of the ancient Irish tradition of hospitality, she kidnapped the young heir of the family. He was later returned on the promise that the gates would always be open at the dinner hour and an extra place laid at the table for an unexpected guest. Although this legend could not be factually verified, to this day this tradition still holds. An extra place is always set at the dinner table and the gates are always open to the public.

38. It may be necessary to seek professional help and/or support programmes.

39. The theme of love exists within all of the major religions. Scripture encourages us to 'Love the Lord your God with all your heart and with all your soul and with all your mind and with all your strength. Love your neighbour as thy self. There is no commandment greater than these.' From the Gospel of St Mark, 12:30–31.

40. Twist, Lynne, *The Soul of Money*, W.W. Norton and Co. (2003), pp. 67–74.

41. 'And God said, Let us make man in our image, after our likeness' and 'So God created man in His own image, in the image of God He created him; male and female He created them': 1:26 and 1:27, quoted from the King James version of the Book of Genesis.

42. Third verse of the King James version of the Book of Genesis, as previously quoted in this book: 'And God said, Let there be light: and there was light.'

43. Marianne Williamson, *A Return to Love*, HarperCollins (1992), p. 165.

44. Allen, James, *As a Man Thinketh*, Rise of Douai Publishing (2013, first published 1903), p. 29.

45. This is an old Irish blessing.

ACKNOWLEDGEMENTS

A heartfelt thank you to my family and friends and those near and dear to me for your loving support every step of the way while writing this book. Most especially to Dr Carol Smyth and Daniel Dooher I give thanks for challenging me to go deeper, explore further and move beyond limitations. From the inception of this book, through the numerous drafts to the final editing, your flashes of inspiration and great humour have made it an absolute joy to work together. Thanks also to Carol for providing medical advice in the relevant sections of this book.

To Marianne Gunn O'Connor, I am grateful for your generosity of spirit in playing an intrinsic role in the publication of *Taking Heaven Lightly* by introducing me to Ciara Considine, commissioning editor at Hachette Books Ireland. To Ciara Considine, you have been fantastic to work with and I feel blessed to have been able to place this book in your trusted hands. Thank you for keeping the integrity of the message of the Eternal Light throughout the pages. To all the team at Hachette Books Ireland, especially Breda Purdue, I greatly appreciate your guidance through the maze of the publishing world.

Thank you to the medical staff at both St Columcille's Hospital and Beaumont Hospital for your medical expertise and kindness during my illness. I especially thank Kevin Deitrich, for your professional assistance at a time when I was unable to manage for myself and most needed it.

I wish to express gratitude to Dr Deepak Chopra, Marianne Williamson, Roma Downey, Mark Burnett, Dr Christine Ranck, Michael Gelb and my friends at the United Nations SRC Enlightenment Society, the Conscious Capitalism Institute and the Society of Enlightened Entrepreneurs for your inspirational guidance. At times when I wavered on this path, your strength kept me going.

Thank you for the generous support I received over the past few years from: former Ambassador of Ireland to the United States, H.E. Michael Collins and Mrs Marie Collins; current Ambassador of Ireland to the United States, H.E. Anne Anderson; Ambassador Jean Kennedy Smith; Secretary General of the Department of Foreign Affairs Mr Niall Burgess and Mrs Marie Morgan-Burgess; Ambassador Noel Kilkenny and Mrs Hanora Kilkenny; Ambassador Elizabeth Frawley Bagley. Thanks to Counsellor Michael Lonergan and Mrs Kirsty Lonergan, Loretta Brennan Glucksman, Sir James Galway, Bill Whelan, Moya Brennan, Sean Mahon, Prof. Martin Curley, Dr Susan Jeffords, Anthony Murphy, Ciara Bradley, Carol Tansley, Susan and Vivian Davis, Michele Ryan, Christy O'Connor Jnr, Claire Haugh, Mary Rose Glennon and John Fitzpatrick OBE.

To all the journalists, editors and radio presenters who assisted me in New York and Washington, D.C., a huge thank you from the bottom of my heart for your tremendous support. Thanks to the Irish-American community, the Ireland Funds, the American Irish Historical Society, Irish Repertory Theatre and Irish Arts Center and the Irish business networks, including the Ireland–US Council, Ireland Inc., Irish Chamber of Commerce USA, Irish Business Organization, Irish International Business Network and Irish Network. I would also like to thank the National Concert Hall in Ireland, the Irish-American Heritage Museum, Glucksman Ireland House and Anam Cara Gallery in the United States for displaying my artwork.

I am grateful to Michael Kelleher and his staff at Bray Library. Thank you, Michael – whenever I requested an out-of-print, limited edition of an obscure Irish book, you would search in your collection of old manuscripts and invariably find it. I would especially like to thank Tony Bohan at the library of Trinity College Dublin for helping me with my research. Also, thanks to Prof. William Kingston of Trinity College Dublin for your encouragement at the early stages of developing my art.

My thanks to Prof. George Eogan for generously sharing your wealth of knowledge gained from over 50 years of directing archaeological excavations at Knowth, in the Boyne Valley region of Ireland. George has made many amazing archaeological discoveries which have forever changed our perception of the Neolithic sites in the Boyne Valley and our understanding of the culture of the people who built them, not just in Ireland but throughout Europe. I am also indebted to you for making the time in your busy schedule to bring me on a field trip to Knowth, one of the most important Neolithic sites in Ireland, and for explaining every facet of this wondrous site in minute detail.

To archaeologist Helen Roche, I am grateful for your patience as you guided me through the intricacies of some of the megalithic sites throughout Ireland. There is nothing like getting covered from head to toe in mud, crawling through the passageways and squeezing between huge standing stones to really grasp the true meaning of our ancient heritage. I also greatly appreciate your input into the archaeological section of this book. Similarly, I thank Dr Frank Prendergast and Dr Robert Hensey for your fascinating interpretations of the astronomical and light phenomena at the Neolithic sites in Ireland and for helping me to portray these ideas clearly. I wish to give special thanks to Robert Hensey for reading the draft versions of the archaeology chapter and for encouraging me to write about my experiences of these ancient sites.

With gratitude I would like to acknowledge all the individuals throughout the centuries who have collated a vast quantity of old Irish literature. Many scholars and professionals have devoted their lives to bringing this knowledge to light. Without their dedication much of this archaic culture would have been lost or never discovered. To Dr John Carey, from the Department of Early and Medieval Irish at University College Cork, I give thanks for generously sharing your understanding of old Irish literature. I wish to thank you for reading the draft manuscript of the section on ancient Irish legends. Trying to comprehend the meaning of these beautiful and intriguing tales is like entering into the 'Otherworld', as one begins to question and separate what is real from what is unreal. Your expert guidance was invaluable on this journey. Also, Dr Maureen Concannon, Dr Máirín Ní Núalláin, and the founders and organisers of the Bard School, Sandy Dunlop and Ellen O'Malley Dunlop, I thank for the passion with which you have brought these ancient myths to life over the past 20 years.

I am grateful to Jason Horseman and Dr Richard Batley, Christ's College, Cambridge, for explaining the fundamentals of physics to a non-physicist. This was not an easy task but one for which I am very grateful.

Thank you to my cousins Mick Fitzpatrick, Aine Meek, Tom Linehan and Tom O'Brien for your detailed research into our family genealogy and bringing our past back to life.

Prof. Lizbeth Goodman, founder of SMARTlab and president of Safetynet. I thank for your tireless dedication to making the impossible possible and the unimaginable a reality. Your extraordinary vision of what this world could be inspires me daily to not only follow my dreams but to create them anew, each and every day.

To Dr Bruce Greyson, one of the leading experts in the field of NDE research in the United States, I give my sincerest thanks. When I had the idea to write this book, I approached you for your advice because I was unsure if I had anything of value to add to the information already available about NDEs. I hope that this book comes close to the one that you envisioned I would write.

I greatly appreciate the kindness of an exceptional group of friends on both sides of the Atlantic who constantly encourage me and bring so much joy to my life. I also give thanks to the women in my meditation group in Dublin for your gracious presence in my life. A special acknowledgement for Betty Cosgrave; your angelic presence always guides me to soar, reaching new and unexplored heights. To Heather Altland De Diaz, I am grateful for your invaluable insights which steer me on the right course in life. And, Laurence Crowley CBE, thank you for inspiring me in life with your combination, in equal parts, of humour, humility and wisdom.

Finally, no words could ever express my gratitude for the Divine Wisdom I have received, and continue to receive, in my life. For all the support from the visible and invisible realms, I give thanks with the fullness of my heart and soul, for this awakening to the truth of the pure love of Universal Consciousness and the beauty of the eternal light.

Giving Back

Over the past few years, one of my greatest joys has been to donate artwork to raise funds for various charities. I have intentionally focused on charities that strive to improve the quality of life for people of all ages by providing hope and inspiration, especially during the most challenging of times. Please see www.RoisinFitzpatrick.com for further details.